FDR's NEW DEAL

The famous NRA Blue Eagle emblem

Don Lawson

FDR's NEW DEAL

ILLUSTRATED WITH PHOTOGRAPHS

Thomas Y. Crowell   New York

Copyright © 1979 by Don Lawson

All rights reserved. Printed in the United States of America. No part of this book may be used or reproduced in any manner whatsoever without written permission except in the case of brief quotations embodied in critical articles and reviews. For information address Thomas Y. Crowell, 10 East 53 Street, New York, N. Y. 10022. Published simultaneously in Canada by Fitzhenry & Whiteside Limited, Toronto.
Designed by Trish Parcell

LIBRARY OF CONGRESS CATALOGING IN PUBLICATION DATA
Lawson, Don   FDR's New Deal.
SUMMARY: Discusses the administration, legislation, and personalities of Roosevelt's New Deal, a sweeping program which attempted to bring the United States out of a severe economic depression.
Bibliography
Index
1. United States—Politics and government—1933–1945—Juvenile literature. 2. Roosevelt, Franklin Delano, Pres. U.S., 1882–1945—Juvenile literature. [1. United States—Politics and government—1933–1945. 2. Roosevelt, Franklin Delano, Pres, U.S.,1882–1945] I. Title.
E806.L37   1979   320.9'73'0917   78-4775
ISBN 0-690-03953-0

Frontispiece: Wide World Photos

*To my mother
with love and gratitude*

ALSO BY DON LAWSON

The Young People's History of America's Wars Series

The Colonial Wars
The American Revolution
The War of 1812
The United States in the Indian Wars
The United States in the Mexican War
The United States in the Civil War
The United States in the Spanish-American War
The United States in World War I
The United States in World War II
The United States in the Korean War

Contents

1	Boom and Bust	1
2	The Great Depression Begins	12
3	A New Deal for the American People	23
4	Nothing to Fear but Fear Itself	36
5	The New Deal's First Hundred Days	43
6	First Lady of the Cabinet	57
7	Felix Frankfurter's Happy Hot Dogs	78
8	Hunger Is Not Debatable	92
9	End of the New Deal Honeymoon	103
10	The Supreme Court Fight	114
11	End of the New Deal	127
12	World War II Begins	133
	Bibliography	141
	Index	143

CHAPTER ONE

Boom and Bust

ON AN OCTOBER day in 1929, a day that was as brilliant as a newly minted proof coin, the New York stock market collapsed. The actual date was Thursday, October 24, 1929, a day that would be long remembered as Black Thursday. There soon followed the greatest financial panic and most serious economic depression in American history.

Between October's Black Thursday and the middle of the following month, financial losses on the New York stock market amounted to some thirty billion dollars—a sum twice the size of the United States national debt at that time. It was also just about the same amount of money the United States had spent taking part in World War I, which had come to an end slightly more than a decade earlier.

Partially as an aftermath of the war there had been a period of great economic prosperity in the 1920s. This boom period came to be known as the Roaring Twenties. But the war was also largely responsible for the economic collapse of 1929, which ushered in the Great Depression of the 1930s and led to President Franklin Delano Roosevelt's history-making New Deal.

During World War I, America's farmers had produced record food supplies for the United States and for the many nations of Europe engaged in the conflict. After the war Europe's farmers returned to tilling their fields and raising food animals, and the need for American food supplies abruptly ended. As a result huge surpluses glutted the American market. Wheat, corn, oats, lard, butter, and eggs filled American granaries, grain elevators, and warehouses to overflowing. With each new crop these bulging surpluses grew, and prices fell drastically. In addition, there was an enormous surplus of cotton which had been in great demand during the war and now rotted in the fields.

In the 1920s farmers made up almost half the population of the United States. These included farm owners, tenant farmers, sharecroppers, and hired farm workers. When the products produced by this huge work force backed up in the marketplace because they

Boom and Bust

could not be sold, it meant that half the nation's population could not afford to buy the machinery and supplies it needed. As a result, factories would soon close, and mass unemployment was bound to result.

But during most of the 1920s this "silent depression" was felt only in the farming regions of the United States. People fled the farm belt at the rate of six hundred thousand a year and moved into the cities. There and elsewhere outside the farm belt there was such a pent-up demand for every kind of goods and service, as a result of "doing without" and the nationwide spirit of self-sacrifice during the war, that a tremendous economic boom took place. Few people seemed to realize that it was a boom built on quicksand, or if they realized it, they did not seem to care.

For the war had also caused a great change in people's moral attitudes. Most young Americans had gone into the war in a spirit of romantic adventure. Woodrow Wilson, America's wartime President, had added a spiritual quality to this adventure by saying that America was fighting "to make the world safe for democracy." After the war, however, a feeling of bitterness and cynicism began to set in as a reaction to the senseless slaughter that had taken place on the Western Front.

Refusing to realize that the automatic machine gun and other modern defensive weapons had completely changed the nature of war, the leaders of the Allies and the Central Powers had sent millions of men to their death to gain only a few yards of useless ground. This senseless mass slaughter had gone on for years, wiping out an entire generation of young men from England, France, Germany, and many other countries of Europe. Fortunately, the United States had entered the war late and took part in relatively few battles, so American losses could be numbered in the thousands rather than the millions. Nevertheless, each death and each maimed man was a permanent reminder of the war's futility—especially since it had apparently settled little and gained even less for both victors and vanquished.

In its reaction against the war America turned its back on Europe and returned to its long-standing isolationist attitude. It not only refused to join the new world peace organization, the League of Nations, sponsored by Woodrow Wilson, but it also turned away from Wilson's political party, the Democrats. The Democrats were blamed by many for getting the nation into the war. Now what was wanted was a party that would guarantee a return to peace and prosperity and a return to "normalcy." This, the Republicans promised.

A series of three Republican Presidents followed Wilson in office—Warren G. Harding, Calvin Coolidge, and Herbert Hoover. It was Harding who popularized the term "normalcy," but he died in office, and it was under his successor, Coolidge, and the man who succeeded Coolidge, Hoover, that normalcy returned to the land. Actually it was a decade of unprecedented prosperity.

The end of the enormous costs of the war allowed both the national debt and federal taxes to be reduced. The return to isolationism meant increased protective tariffs which, temporarily at least, seemed to aid American manufacturers in making money. Mass production came into its own, to turn out such new products as radios, automobiles, refrigerators, sound motion pictures, and airplanes. Isolationism also resulted in the restriction of immigration, making more jobs available to American citizens. The nation's roads were greatly improved, and a building boom swept the country. In the cities new skyscrapers were erected, and in the suburbs and countryside, whole new plots of individual homes sprang up in what had been barren fields. The homes in these subdivisions were equipped with all of the new "modern conveniences"—electricity, indoor plumbing, refrigerators, radios—and most families had their first automobiles. Prosperity, it seemed, was a permanent part of American life, and it was true that most people were living better lives materially than ever before. While there was more of almost everything for everybody, there was less illiteracy, less poverty, less malnutrition, and less slum housing.

There was also more personal freedom, especially among America's women. In 1920 the Nineteenth Amendment to the Constitution was passed, giving women the right to vote. This landmark law was the highwater mark for the women's liberation movement of its day, and it signaled a radical change in American society. Women expressed their independence in numerous ways. They stopped letting their hair grow naturally long, having it cut in short "boyish bobs." They also began to smoke cigarettes openly in public. In addition, sexual freedom for women as well as men became more commonly accepted than ever before in American history.

Behind such apparent freedom, however, the United States also clung to some degree to its traditional Puritan ways. In 1919 the Eighteenth Amendment to the Constitution had been passed, establishing national prohibition. This made the sale of alcoholic beverages illegal in the United States. It was thought that this law would eliminate both the unsavory saloon as well as all the evils of drink. But the American public—not only its "flaming youth" who were filling the nation's schools and colleges in unprecedented numbers, but also its older generation—flagrantly disregarded prohibition. So-called speakeasies opened behind secret doors in place of the old saloons, and the illegal manufacture, importation, and sale of bootleg liquor gave rise to a whole new industry dominated by gangsters and underworld hoodlums.

Despite the wild prosperity of the 1920s, there were serious problems. First of all, there was the chronic farm problem—it got no better under any of the three postwar Republican Presidents. (President Coolidge, who had grown up on a farm, ignored the problem with the comment, "The business of America is business.") Second, both coal mining and textile manufacturing never fully recovered from the sudden cutoff in foreign markets that occurred at the end of World War I. Third, there was the nationwide speculation in the stock market.

No one has ever satisfactorily explained the stock-market mania that swept the United States in the late 1920s. Part of it was due to a reaction against the war. Part of it was due to many Americans' desire to get rich quick. And part was due to easy credit. Stocks could be bought on margin—that is, a customer only had to put up 10 or 15 percent of the actual purchase price of a stock and the stock broker would loan him the rest. If the stock went up, the customer sold it, paid off the rest of the original cost of the stock, and pocketed a neat profit. Usually, however, this profit wasn't pocketed but reinvested in a new speculative stock—again on margin. Trouble occurred only when a stock went *down* in price after it had been purchased. Then the broker would ask the customer for more money on margin. But between 1926 and 1929 it seemed that no stocks were ever going to do anything but go up, no matter what their original purchase price had been, and the scramble to get into the market became epidemic. To make investment even easier, brokerage offices opened in every town, village, and hamlet across the land. These sometimes amounted to only a bare-walled cubicle with a lone broker and a half-dozen telephones, but they drew customers nonetheless. Such "bucket shops" or "boiler factories" often sold unknown stocks and even nonexistent ones.

Not everyone in America was in the market, of course, but most banks were—those in small as well as large towns. This came about by brokers borrowing money (call money) to pay for stocks that they were buying for their customers on margin. Call money often earned as much as 20 percent interest, and few bankers could resist such a bonanza. The amount of this call money used to purchase stocks became so huge, in fact, that by September of 1929—a month before the Wall Street crash—it amounted to half the size of the United States national debt.

Although not everyone was in the market, most Americans were keenly aware of its feverish activity and perhaps were secretly wishing that they could get in on the paper fortunes that were being made. Barbers, beauty-shop operators, taxicab drivers all spoke as knowledgeably of the latest stock-market reports as they did of local events or of the latest gangland killings among the bootleggers. Gains—always they seemed to be gains—in the popular stocks of the day made the newspaper headlines or received special attention in radio broadcasts. Everybody seemed to know somebody who had invested a thousand dollars in some new stock offering last month that was worth ten thousand dollars today.

Investment trusts were also created to attract the more timid investor. These were set up by companies that owned stock in other companies and were supposedly run by wise Wall Street financiers. A person could invest in these for ten or fifteen dollars a share and then rake in a profit when all of the companies in the trust made money. Some of these investment trusts were backed by the most reliable names in the country—J. P. Morgan Company was one; others were backed by totally unknown operators who eventually proved to be nothing more than confidence men. Nevertheless, customers bought their shares and clamored for more, so that by 1929 there were literally billions of dollars invested in investment trusts.

As the market continued to climb, there were a few financiers and government leaders who urged caution, but most were so deeply involved with their own investments that they, too, threw caution to the winds. Even President Hoover and his Secretary of the Treasury, Andrew W. Mellon, refused to sound any national alarm, although both later claimed they had foreseen the crash. The United States Federal Reserve Board did issue occasional warnings against dangerous speculation, but these warnings were feeble and generally went unheeded.

Finally, in early September, prices on the New York Stock Exchange began to slide. But there had been occasional downturns before, and the market had always recovered. Roger Babson, however, one of the nation's most astute financiers, announced that disaster was at hand and a major depression would soon follow. Again, few heeded.

But the slide in prices continued, with occasional upward adjustments, all through the month of September and into October. On Black Thursday, October 24, disaster did indeed strike. Prices plunged wildly on the market, and nothing, it seemed, could stop them. Even when a group of the nation's leading bankers formed a pool of ninety million dollars to buy stocks and stop the plunge, the delay in falling prices was only temporary.

At this point President Hoover and other government officials began to issue statements from Washington about the fundamental soundness of the nation's economy, but these had no effect. Thousands upon thousands of investors had seen their life savings wiped out; banks, also by the thousands, faced ruin.

Tuesday, October 29, was equally black. On that

day almost twenty million shares of stock were sold, most at severe losses. This was a record that would not be matched until the 1960s. Investment trusts by the hundreds collapsed. Now it was at long last clear; prosperity was not a permanent way of life in America as some had come to believe. In fact quite the opposite soon seemed to be true: economic depression was more apt to be a permanent part of most people's lives.

It was out of this historic period of unprecedented boom and bust—or, as some people called it, "Boom and Doom"—that President Franklin D. Roosevelt's New Deal for America would be born.

CHAPTER TWO

The Great Depression Begins

THE ECONOMIC DEPRESSION did not set in immediately after the stock-market crash and the panic in Wall Street. There were, after all, still many people who had money. But gradually even people with money began to refuse to spend it. This caused a chain reaction. Soon manufacturers were finding little or no market for their goods. They in turn laid off employees and shut down their plants. The people who were thrown out of work were forced to economize because what little money they had would soon run out. This forced more and more businesses to close. In addition, the farm problem, which had been bad for years, got steadily worse.

The Great Depression Begins

Government officials in Washington maintained their optimistic outlook, at least publicly. So did many financiers and Wall Street speculators. In fact in the spring of 1930 there was an upsurge in stock prices, causing President Hoover to observe happily, "We have now passed the worst, and we shall rapidly recover." But in a few short weeks the "little bull market," as this temporary stock-market recovery was called, collapsed, and the Great Depression set in in earnest.

Soon, men without jobs were standing in breadlines and lining up before charity-sponsored soup kitchens in all of the major cities of the United States. In New York City alone by the end of 1930 there were more than eighty breadlines serving eighty-five thousand free meals a day. Some jobless men sold pencils and shoelaces on street corners. Others sold apples at five cents each. They obtained the apples from the International Apple Shippers' Association, which was trying every possible means to get rid of its enormous surplus apple crop.

In 1930 there were some four and a half million unemployed. This number increased to more than five million by 1931 and to more than twelve million by 1932. The population of the United States was about half of what it is today. These figures meant that about one person in every five in the labor force was without a job. In addition, millions of adults were only working part time. The average weekly pay for a person working in manufacturing was about twenty-five dollars in 1930. In 1932 it had dropped to about sixteen dollars. The average family income was sixteen hundred dollars a year. Only one family in five had an annual income of as much as three thousand dollars.

The situation in rural areas was equally bad. By 1932 farm prices had fallen so low that it cost farmers money to raise and market their crops. Wheat was selling for thirty-nine cents a bushel, corn for thirty-three cents a bushel, and cotton for six cents a pound. Violence broke out in many farm states. In Iowa, members of the Farm Holiday Association put up roadblocks to stop farmers from bringing their crops to market. It was thought that the scarcity resulting from such action might drive up prices, but this effort did not work. In Wisconsin, dairy farmers dumped their milk or fed it to their hogs rather than sell it at a loss. When farm auctions were held to dispose of the farms and equipment of bankrupt farmers, their neighbors threatened auctioneers with bodily harm if anything was sold. When sales were held despite these threats, the sale items were bought for ridiculously low prices and returned free of charge to the bankrupt farmers by their neighbors.

Violence also began to erupt in industrial areas. When out-of-work laborers in Dearborn, Michigan, staged a protest march against a Ford automobile

The Great Depression Begins

plant, police fired on them. Four demonstrators were killed, and some fifty were wounded. Workers took part in food riots in Oklahoma City and Minneapolis. Similar outbreaks occurred elsewhere, and soon a spirit of revolution seemed to threaten the nation. Generally speaking, however, the great majority of the people remained peaceful though despairing.

Also in 1932 a so-called Bonus Army marched on Washington. The Bonus Army was made up of veterans of the United States Army from World War I. In 1924 Congress had passed a law providing these several million veterans with insurance policies to be paid off for their cash-surrender value in 1945. In the heart of the Great Depression, out-of-work veterans began to demand that they receive the money immediately. When they were refused, the veterans decided to march on Washington, D.C., and personally lay siege to President Hoover and Congress. By the spring of 1932 some twenty thousand veterans—many brought their wives and children with them—were camped in and around Washington, mainly on the mud flats of the Potomac River.

The siege was a peaceful one, even when the Senate defeated a bill to pay the bonus. Finally, however, President Hoover ordered contingents of the regular army to drive out their former comrades-in-arms. The man who led the armed march against the unarmed veterans was United States Army Chief of Staff Douglas MacArthur. MacArthur was assisted by two company-grade officers, George S. Patton, Jr., and Dwight D. Eisenhower.

At bayonet point the Bonus Army was chased out of Washington, and the "Hooverville" shacks in which they had been living were burned to the ground. Its members had to wait until the spring of 1936 to receive their money. President Hoover did offer to provide money to pay the veterans' train fare back to their homes. Some took advantage of this offer; most did not.

Later, when Franklin D. Roosevelt became President, many of these same veterans were put to work on a government-funded highway-construction project across the Florida keys to Key West. In 1935, before this Overseas Highway could be completed, a hurricane struck the area, killing many of the veterans. When the highway was completed in the late 1930s, a monument was erected to their memory along the right of way.

Even before the Bonus March, President Hoover was a man much disliked by many Americans. This was unfortunate, and for the most part undeserved. He just happened to be the wrong President at the wrong time. Actually, Hoover was probably one of the most able and humane men who ever served in the office. The economic climate of the times was, however, against him. So were his looks and dress. An extremely serious, even cold-looking man, he always wore a high starched collar that made him seem even more austere and set him off from the common man.

Hoover's public-service record was remarkable. During World War I he had been in charge of Belgian and French relief. Millions of people in Belgium and the part of France that was occupied by the Germans were faced with starvation because of the war. Hoover's relief committee saved these people from hardship and starvation by shipping them a total of five million tons of food and clothing—most of it from the United States. For this work, as well as for all his other work in public office, Hoover never accepted any salary. An independently wealthy man from his civilian work as an engineer, he turned all of his government salary—even that which he received as President—back to the government or contributed it to charity.

Hoover was a great believer in private charity. He did not believe in direct federal aid to the unemployed. He thought that such aid—the dole as he called it, after the British term for unemployment relief—would weaken the independence and self-reliance of the individuals receiving it. If such aid were really needed, he felt, it should be handled at the local government level or by private charity. Federal aid to the poor was, Hoover said, socialistic and would lead to the destruction of democracy. "We cannot squander ourselves into prosperity," Hoover told reporters in 1932. He also thought that if people would stop talking about hard times, they would go away. "Prosperity," he insisted, "is just around the corner." In time this latter statement became something of a bitter joke among the unemployed.

Nevertheless, as the Depression grew worse, Hoover did begin to realize that some form of economic assistance was necessary to get the country back on the track to recovery. To this end in 1932 he succeeded in getting Congress to create the Reconstruction Finance Corporation (RFC). The RFC was authorized to make strictly limited loans to the states for relief and public welfare. Its most important role, however, was to loan money to banks, industries, loan companies, insurance companies, railroads, and certain other businesses. Some two billion dollars was loaned out by the RFC with the idea that this money would eventually "trickle down" from the men at the top of the financial structure of the country to the unemployed at the bottom. But as the Depression deepened, it became obvious that the people at the bottom couldn't possibly wait for the trickle-down theory to work. Very few of them had received even a drop of trickle-down money by late 1932. What was needed, Hoover's critics insisted, was direct federal aid, not only to businessmen but also to farmers and unemployed men and women everywhere.

Consequently Hoover's name became a harsh joke

to the hungry and homeless. City people who were forced out of their homes because of mortgage foreclosures or because they couldn't pay their rent lived in packing-crate houses and other makeshift dwelling places in shantytowns at the edges of cities. These shantytowns, like that of the Bonus Army in Washington, were always called Hoovervilles. Poor and hungry rural people in the West and Southwest killed and ate jackrabbits which they called Hoover hogs. Many jobless people who couldn't afford to pay for transportation to different areas to look for work frequently moved about the country by riding like hoboes aboard freight cars. The hoboes called these freight cars side-door Pullmans, after the plush railroad sleeping cars invented by George Pullman that were on all the nation's first-class passenger trains. The new transients called them Hoover Pullmans.

This transient population aboard Hoover Pullmans had become a small army by late 1932, estimated at more than a million. Included in its ranks were a quarter of a million young boys and girls, according to estimates made by the Children's Bureau. Many of the girls in this army of drifters disguised themselves as boys to try to prevent sexual attacks. Thousands of boys and girls also hitchhiked about the country, some looking for jobs, others just because there was nothing else to do.

Perhaps the most serious immediate problem

Hoover and his administration had to face as the Depression grew worse had to do with the nation's banks. Following the stock-market collapse they began to close, first a few and then by the dozen and finally by the hundreds. In 1931 and 1932 almost a thousand banks across the country shut their doors. As each bank closed, the life savings of its depositors were lost, since there was no federal bank insurance covering deposits in those days. This threw an enormous additional burden on the country's failing economy, which was steadily moving toward complete collapse.

It was perhaps the banking crisis more than anything else that made Americans come to the conclusion that the nation needed a new President. The first rumblings threatening the overturn of the long Republican regime were heard during the congressional and state elections in the autumn of 1930, when there were many Democratic victories. Democrats took control of the House of Representatives and were evenly divided with the Republicans in the Senate. This made Hoover realize that he would soon be faced with a hostile Congress. Among the victors in the state elections was Franklin D. Roosevelt, who was elected to a second term as governor of New York by an overwhelming margin. Already there were those who were predicting that the handsome and popular governor of New York would be the nation's next President.

By the end of 1932 the nation was truly in desperate straits. While official estimates gave the number of unemployed as twelve million, there were other estimates that said that this figure should more accurately be seventeen million. And many men and women had been out of work since 1929. The jobless rate continued to climb. Unemployment rates climbed to 80 percent in some cities. The steel industry was operating at only a small fraction of its normal capacity. More and more farmers lost their farms. Banks kept closing at an alarming rate, while those few people who had money hoarded it against what looked like a darker future. For the first time in American history, people throughout the country were starving to death in relatively large numbers. Several thousand cases of "death by malnutrition" were reported in the major cities. New York City hospitals alone reported more than one hundred cases of starvation in 1932, and there was only speculation regarding how many similar cases had gone unrecorded. And this was the case, despite the fact that milk was selling for ten cents a quart, bread for seven cents a loaf, butter for twenty-three cents a pound, eggs for twenty cents a dozen, and hamburger for fifteen cents a pound.

Despite the Depression, Herbert Hoover was nominated by the Republicans early in June of 1932 for reelection to the Presidency. Actually they had no other choice, since to have nominated someone else would have been an open admission that the Hoover administration was a Republican failure.

The Democratic nomination for the Presidency was,

as Franklin Roosevelt's campaign manager James A. Farley put it, "a horse race." The three leading candidates were Alfred E. Smith, John Nance Garner, and Roosevelt. Smith was a former governor of New York and also a former presidential candidate who had been defeated by Hoover in the 1928 election. Garner was a popular congressman from Texas and the current Speaker of the House of Representatives. In his second term as governor of New York, Roosevelt had made a name for himself as the champion of the common man.

Before the Democratic Convention met in the Chicago Stadium in late June, Jim Farley and another Roosevelt aide, Louis McHenry Howe, had persuaded most of the delegates to nominate Roosevelt. On the first three ballots a simple majority of the delegates did vote for him, but a two-thirds majority was needed to secure the nomination. Fearing that Smith's and Garner's backers might combine their votes against Roosevelt and deadlock the convention, Farley finally succeeded in getting the Texas delegation to switch its vote to Roosevelt. In return Garner was promised the vice-presidential nomination. On the sweltering evening of July 1, 1932, Franklin Delano Roosevelt, or FDR as he was popularly known, received the Democratic nomination for the Presidency of the United States.

CHAPTER THREE

A New Deal for the American People

As soon as Roosevelt received word in New York that he had been nominated, he made the first of many bold moves that were to mark his campaign and service as President. He chartered an airplane and flew to Chicago to make his acceptance speech. Until then, it had always been the custom for the presidential nominee to remain at home until he was informed and then release a statement to the press. But FDR, in a propeller-driven, trimotored Ford plane known as a Tin Goose, chose to fly to Chicago despite tradition and despite foul weather.

Roosevelt's acceptance speech was also bold. It was the kind of challenge that both the delegates and the American people wanted to hear. In it he said:

I pledge you—I pledge myself to a new deal for the American people. Let us all here assembled constitute ourselves prophets of a new order of competence and of courage. This is more than a political campaign; it is a call to arms. Give me your help, not to win votes alone, but to win in this crusade to restore America to its own people.

Afterward vice-presidential nominee Garner confidently told FDR, "All you have to do to win is stay alive."

But there were many observers who disagreed with Garner. One was political pundit and highly regarded newspaper columnist Walter Lippmann. "Franklin D. Roosevelt," Lippmann wrote, "is no crusader. He is no tribune of the people. He is a pleasant and amiable man who, without any important qualifications for the office, would very much like to be President."

In the campaign ahead, Roosevelt was determined to convince the American people just how wrong Lippmann and others like him were. And FDR was determined also to wage not a "back porch" campaign—one in which he merely stayed at home and issued statements—but an active and aggressive one. Roosevelt had been a fighter ever since returning to the political wars following a crippling attack of infantile paralysis, and he knew that one of the worst enemies a politician could have was overconfidence, such as that expressed by his running mate, Garner.

A New Deal for the American People

Franklin Delano Roosevelt was born on January 30, 1882, at Hyde Park, New York. His father, James, was a prosperous railroad official and landowner. His mother, Sara, was a member of the wealthy Delano family. James was in his fifties and a widower when he and twenty-six-year-old Sara Delano were married in 1880. He had had one son, James, Jr., by his first wife. James Junior was eighteen when his half brother Franklin was born.

Although young Franklin was reared as an only child and taught by tutors until he was fourteen, he was not a spoiled boy. Both his mother and father insisted that he study hard, work hard, and play hard, but that he behave himself and respect his elders at all times. Nevertheless, his parents' wealth did give him many advantages. By the time he was in his early teens, he had been to Europe eight times. Many of his summers were spent at Campobello, a rocky Canadian island off the coast of Maine. Here Franklin first learned his love of sailing, a love that lasted all his life. As a boy he also began to collect stamps. This, too, proved to be a lifelong hobby.

Franklin entered Groton, a private boarding school, at the age of fourteen; he then attended Harvard and later studied law in New York City. At Groton he was a good student, managed the baseball team, and was a member of the debating team.

At Harvard young Franklin again made good

grades, and was an editor of the student newspaper, the *Crimson*. He was unsuccessful in his attempt to make the varsity crew, but took an active part in intramural athletics, and later became very partial to golf. While he was still in college, Franklin's father died, and his mother came to live in Boston so she could be near her only son.

After his graduation Franklin entered the Columbia Law School. While he was still a law student, he and Anna Eleanor Roosevelt were married on March 17, 1905. Eleanor and Franklin were distant cousins. They were also both related to Theodore Roosevelt, who was then President of the United States and a man whom Franklin greatly admired. President Roosevelt attended the wedding ceremony, during which he gave the bride away. For many years afterward, Franklin and his wife laughed about the fact that nobody at the ceremony seemed to pay any attention to them and seemed only to be interested in the presence of President Theodore Roosevelt.

In 1906, during Franklin's second year in law school, his wife gave birth to their first child, a daughter, named Anna Eleanor after her mother. The next year a son, James, was born.

Franklin did not complete law school but passed his bar examination in 1907. He then joined a New York City law firm. He was still inspired by President Roosevelt, however, and like him wanted to take an active part in politics. Despite the fact that the district in which he lived, Hyde Park, was a Republican stronghold, Franklin decided to run for state senator on the Democratic ticket in 1910. To everyone's surprise he scored a substantial victory.

At Albany, the state capital, FDR became the leader of a group of young Democrats who were fighting against the political machine known as Tammany Hall. Tammany had decided that one of the machine politicians, William F. "Blue-eyed Billie" Sheehan, should be elected to the United States Senate. Roosevelt and his followers did not think Sheehan was qualified for the job, and they successfully blocked his election. The party bosses began to sit up and take notice of this young senator from Hyde Park who wasn't content merely to sit back and rest on the magic name of Roosevelt. He seemed in fact to be determined to make a name for himself. In 1912 FDR was elected to a second term as state senator, tallying a larger majority than he had two years earlier.

Also in 1912 FDR was a delegate to the Democratic National Convention. He strongly supported the nomination of Woodrow Wilson, his new idol, for President. When Wilson was nominated and then elected, the new President called FDR to Washington as Assistant Secretary of the Navy. He served in that post under Josephus Daniels from 1913 to 1920, taking brief time out in 1914 for an unsuccessful bid to obtain the Democratic nomination as United States senator from New York.

When World War I began, FDR and Daniels worked tirelessly to ready the United States Navy for the conflict. After America entered the war, FDR played a key role in breaking the back of Germany's submarine warfare. He did so by urging the construction of a fleet of submarine chasers and by suggesting a novel method of blocking off the North Sea to German U-boats by laying down a barrier of mines in the area. The sub chasers and the belt of mines, plus the use of the convoy method by the American and British navies, ended the U-boat threat.

After the war Roosevelt joined Woodrow Wilson's crusading efforts to get the United States to join the League of Nations. When both Wilson's crusade and his health failed, FDR took up the cause. He was one of the leading Democrats who insisted that the party continue to fight for America's entry into the League. As a result FDR was nominated for Vice-President and James M. Cox, governor of Ohio, was nominated for President on the Democratic ticket in the election of 1920.

But this was the postwar election that turned the Democrats out of office and elected the first of the trio of Republican Presidents—Warren G. Harding. Cox and Roosevelt were defeated by the biggest margin in the nation's history up to that time. Roosevelt even failed to carry Hyde Park.

A New Deal for the American People

After this disastrous defeat, FDR spent much of his time practicing law to support his family, which was now a large one. Four more sons had been born since their father's law-school days. Elliott had been born in 1910, Franklin Delano, Jr., in 1914, and John in 1916. One other son died in infancy.

In August 1921, the Roosevelt family was vacationing at Campobello Island. One day FDR took his daughter Anna and two of his sons, Elliott and James, out with him in the family sailboat. While they were sailing, they spotted a forest fire on a nearby island. Immediately they went ashore and helped to put out the blaze. This took several hours. Afterward, to cool off, they all went swimming.

When they returned home, FDR sat in his wet bathing suit for half an hour, reading his mail. Suddenly he suffered a chill. In bed that night he began also to suffer severe pain. The next day he had a fever, and a doctor was called. FDR was ordered to remain in bed. The next day his legs were paralyzed. Within three days he was completely paralyzed from the chest down. He had been stricken with the dread poliomyelitis, or infantile paralysis, which had spread throughout the nation that summer. At first it was feared that the Roosevelt children might also come down with the disease, but none of them seemed to suffer anything but a mild cold.

There now began a grim fight to save FDR's life, a fight that lasted several weeks. When it was finally over, FDR's life was saved, but he was almost a complete cripple. He was not a helpless cripple, however. This he set out to prove almost as soon as he was allowed out of bed.

He still had the full use of the upper part of his body, and he discovered that when he went swimming, the water's buoyancy enabled him to move about quite freely. He determined to swim as much as possible and to practice crawling to strengthen his arms.

"The water put me where I am," FDR told a friend, "and the water has to bring me back."

To carry on his lonely battle, Roosevelt went to Florida, bought a houseboat, and cruised about in search of deserted beaches where he could swim for hours at a time. His lower legs remained shriveled and virtually useless, but his body above the waist grew strong as an athlete's. He soon became such a powerful swimmer that people seeing him in the water could not believe he was a polio victim. Out of the water he had to wear heavy leg braces and be supported by others or use canes in order to stand and walk. But even when he was being moved about in a wheelchair, FDR gave an impression of such physical strength and energy that few people ever thought of him as a cripple.

FDR's continuing efforts to overcome his handicap led him in the fall of 1924 to an old and once-fashionable resort at Warm Springs, Georgia. He found that the warm springs—the temperature of the water was always around 85 degrees—were especially helpful to him, and he felt certain they would benefit others who had been afflicted by polio. Using his own money plus contributions from friends, he established the Georgia Warm Springs Foundation for the care and treatment of polio victims. There were a good many such victims before the discovery of the polio vaccine in the 1950s, which has since all but eliminated this scourge.

FDR maintained a lifelong interest in the foundation. He visited there regularly, even after he became President, and his home at Warm Springs became known as the Little White House. He was particularly sympathetic to the small boys and girls who were polio victims, and they in turn loved him. Affectionately, he called them his polios, and they always called him Uncle Rosy. One of his frequent pastimes was to take several of his polios for rides in the old car the local blacksmith had rigged up with special ropes and pulleys so FDR could operate it completely by hand.

By the mid-1920s Roosevelt was again practicing law in New York City and had recovered from his illness sufficiently to be able to nominate New York Governor Alfred E. Smith for President at the Democratic Convention. FDR's nominating speech, in which he described Al Smith as a "happy warrior," was long remembered by both the politicians and the public.

Smith was not the party's choice that year, but Roosevelt nominated him again in 1928, and that time Smith was selected. Smith then persuaded Roosevelt to run for the New York State governorship. After much debate FDR finally agreed.

During the campaign some of Roosevelt's unscrupulous political opponents began to circulate stories to the effect that polio had damaged his brain. FDR countered by being thoroughly examined by physicians and making public the results of the examination. One well-known doctor even went to the trouble to observe to reporters that a number of famous men had been polio victims as children. One such person was the famous writer Sir Walter Scott, and polio had certainly not impaired Scott's thinking processes. After this such vicious stories died down, but they were renewed from time to time all during FDR's political career, including his campaign for the Presidency in 1932.

In the elections in the autumn of 1928 in which Hoover badly defeated Smith for the Presidency, FDR was elected to his first term as governor of New York by a comfortable majority. During Roosevelt's two terms in the governorship, he sponsored legislation for old-age pensions, unemployment insurance, prison reform, and a shorter work week. When he began his campaign for the Presidency in 1932, these were also the kinds of reform legislation he promised to initiate if he was elected to that high office. Throughout his political career, in fact, FDR's main objective was to help make life better for every man, woman, and child in America.

Often during the 1932 campaign, Roosevelt emphasized his "common man" theme. "If I am elected," he said, "I will not make the mistake Napoleon made at Waterloo. I will not forget the common man—the infantry."

He also continued to emphasize his promise of a New Deal for America. This term had been suggested to Roosevelt by one of his aides, Raymond Moley, as FDR was preparing his acceptance speech to be delivered in Chicago. It immediately appealed to FDR because it echoed the term Square Deal which his cousin Theodore Roosevelt had used to describe his administration when he was President. Moley may have gotten the term from a recently published book by Stuart Chase called *A New Deal*. In any event, the term symbolized a new hope for America in the midst of its worst economic crisis, and as soon as it was uttered, it placed an indelible stamp on FDR's presidential program.

In the end Garner's prediction was right. Although FDR campaigned vigorously, the results of the election appeared to be a foregone conclusion. Hoover campaigned hard, too, but the nation was sick of the Depression and sick of the government's do-nothing policies. The public's attitude was perhaps best expressed by an anonymous jingle that received wide circulation after one of Hoover's talks in which he promised four years of prosperity if he were returned to office. The jingle went:

> I am sure that we are all a debtor for
> Mr. Hoover's delectable metaphor
> When he said that four years
> Would bring balm to our fears
> Which the starving no doubt feel much better for.

In November 1932 Roosevelt won an unprecedented victory of 472 electoral votes to Hoover's 59. The Democrats also won a large majority of the seats in Congress.

Garner's words about Roosevelt only having to stay alive to win took on something of an ominous note some weeks later when FDR visited Miami, Florida. During a public appearance there, an unemployed workman named Giuseppe Zangara tried to assassinate the President-elect. Zangara's revolver shots missed FDR, but wounded Chicago mayor Anthony Cermak, who was in the party with Roosevelt. Cermak later died, and Zangara was executed for the killing.

Cermak's last words were to FDR. "I'm glad it was me instead of you," he said.

A moment after the shots rang out, the crowd that

had gathered to watch Roosevelt and Cermak heard FDR's voice ring out loud and clear: "I'm all right, I'm all right."

The calm strength in his voice gave assurance to the nation that their new leader would react well to any crisis.

CHAPTER FOUR

Nothing to Fear but Fear Itself

BY THE TIME Roosevelt was sworn into office as President, the economic life of the United States was virtually at a standstill. Unfortunately, the President was then inaugurated on March 4, not January 20 as is the case today. This meant that four long months had to pass between Roosevelt's election and his Inauguration.

Meanwhile, as unemployment mounted and more and more banks closed their doors, President Hoover asked Roosevelt to work with him on emergency measures. But FDR refused. He said that without presidential authority he could not take any responsibility. Actually, he so completely disagreed with Hoover's ideas about the causes of the Depression that he saw no point in meeting with him. Hoover believed that recovery was already under way and that the economy should not be tampered with, while Roosevelt believed radical reforms were necessary to put more purchasing power in the hands of the public.

FDR was not idle, however, as he awaited Inauguration Day. He had to wind up his affairs as governor of New York, pick the members of his Cabinet, and work out detailed plans for his New Deal legislation program. To help him in both efforts he asked for suggestions from the members of his so-called Brain Trust.

The idea for a Brain Trust was originally suggested to FDR by his friend and aide, Samuel I. Rosenman, when FDR started his campaign for the Presidency. Rosenman told FDR he would need advisers who knew a great deal about national affairs, and FDR agreed. They decided to pick these advisers from the ranks of university professors. The first person to be recruited was Raymond Moley, a Columbia professor who had worked with FDR on speeches and various New York state problems. Moley and Basil O'Connor, Roosevelt's law partner, recruited the rest. They included Rexford Guy Tugwell and Adolf A. Berle, Jr., two other Columbia University faculty members. Later Hugh Johnson, a government administrator and former army officer, and United States senators James F. Byrnes of South Carolina and Key Pittman of Nevada were added to the group.

FDR called his group of advisers his privy council, but James Kieran, a reporter for *The New York Times,* dubbed them the Brains Trust. This name caught on with the public, but the *s* was usually dropped, and the popular name soon became the Brain Trust.

For a time FDR tried to keep secret the fact that he had a Brain Trust, since he did not think such a group would be popular with the voting public. But their activities became so widely reported in the press that Hugh Johnson said they were "as easy to track as a herd of elephants in six feet of snow."

Selecting a Cabinet occupied much of FDR's time. He definitely did not want a rubber-stamp Cabinet any more than he wanted a rubber-stamp Brain Trust. First of all, of course, he wanted able administrators, but he also wanted people with fresh ideas who were sold on their ideas to the point where they would fight to carry them out. Finally, with the aid of his Brain Trust, FDR selected the following Cabinet: Secretary of State, Cordell Hull; Secretary of the Treasury, William H. Woodin; Secretary of War, George Dern; Secretary of the Navy, Claude A. Swanson; Attorney General, Homer S. Cummings; Secretary of Agriculture, Henry A. Wallace; Secretary of Commerce, Daniel C. Roper; Secretary of the Interior, Harold L. Ickes; Postmaster General, James A. Farley; and Secretary of Labor, Frances Perkins.

Frances Perkins, a social worker from New York and a long-time associate of FDR's when he was governor, was the first woman ever to serve in a presidential Cabinet. Wallace's father had also served as Secretary of Agriculture, under President Harding. Farley, of course, had been FDR's campaign manager, and he was appointed Postmaster General partially to pay off this political debt. But Farley was an extremely able man in his own right and proved to be a strong member of the Cabinet. Woodin died not long after Inauguration Day and was replaced by Henry Morgenthau, Jr., as Secretary of the Treasury.

On January 30, 1933, just a few weeks before Roosevelt was inaugurated, Adolf Hitler became Chancellor of Germany. Germany, too, had been suffering from the effects of the worldwide Depression, and the German people were looking for a savior to lead them out of economic darkness. Ironically, the man they chose would lead their nation to destruction during the course of the next twelve years. The American people now waited to see what course their new leader would embark the nation upon. Hopefully it would lead them out of darkness into light. Eventually Hitler and Roosevelt would lead their nations into the brutal confrontation of World War II.

Inauguration Day, Saturday, March 4, 1933, was a

bleak and blustery day in Washington—cold, dark, windy, and dreary. Occasionally cold rain slashed across the city. Because of the Depression many people had suggested that there be no formal ceremonies. But FDR vetoed this idea. The people, he insisted, needed a little pomp and ceremony to take their mind off their troubles. Furthermore, the coming into office of a new President, he firmly believed, should be a time of celebration. The ceremony, including the parties and balls after the inauguration, was to go on as usual. But the mood of the people was more like that of a nation at war.

Franklin Delano Roosevelt was sworn into office by the Chief Justice of the Supreme Court, Charles Evans Hughes, on the steps of the Capitol at eight minutes after one o'clock. He became the nation's thirty-second President. More than a hundred thousand people gathered on the Capitol grounds to witness the ceremony and hear the inaugural address that followed. Millions more listened over the radio. The speech was memorable. It was delivered in a warm confident voice filled with ringing challenge:

> This is a day of national consecration, and I am certain that my fellow Americans expect that on my induction into the Presidency I will address them with a candor and a decision which the present situation of our nation impels.
> This is preeminently the time to speak the truth, the

Nothing to Fear but Fear Itself

whole truth, frankly and boldly, nor need we shrink from honestly facing the conditions in our country today. This great nation will endure as it has endured, will revive and will prosper.

So, first of all, let me assert my firm belief that the only thing we have to fear is fear itself—nameless, unreasoning, unjustified terror which paralyzes needed efforts to convert retreat into advance. . . .

Roosevelt continued, but the most memorable words of the speech had already been delivered. The line that everyone would remember was "the only thing we have to fear is fear itself." It immediately began to be quoted and is still frequently quoted today. It also went into the history books. The origin of the phrase is interesting. Many people thought that Roosevelt introduced the phrase himself, perhaps borrowing it from an essay by the American essayist and philosopher Henry David Thoreau. But it did not appear in FDR's original handwritten draft of the inaugural address. Raymond Moley, who kept careful notes of all the speeches on which he worked for FDR, later said the phrase was added at the last minute by aide Louis Howe. And Howe, Moley insisted, had never read Thoreau or even heard of him. Moley did recall, however, that the "nothing to fear" phrase appeared in a New York department store's newspaper advertisement, and Howe, who read many newspapers every day, recognized at once how aptly the words fitted the occasion and suggested them to FDR. FDR, who also had a keen eye for a fitting phrase, immediately accepted the phrase's insertion into his inaugural address.

Actually there were many things to fear with the nation's economy in the state it was, but the fact that the new President was going to face them was what the public wanted to hear. And everyone hoped that it was a good omen when, as FDR neared the end of his speech, the sun broke through the overcast skies and shone briefly across the steps and the dome of the Capitol.

Now the nation awaited FDR's promised action.

CHAPTER FIVE

The New Deal's First Hundred Days

ACTION WAS NOT LONG in coming. It began, in fact, the very next day, Sunday, March 5, and continued without letup until mid-June. This was the New Deal's fabled "First Hundred Days," a period of legislative activity unmatched before or since in the nation's history. During this period, prompted by FDR, his Cabinet, and his Brain Trust, Congress passed fifteen major emergency acts. In addition, the tireless President made a dozen speeches, held numerous press conferences and Cabinet meetings, and carried on countless personal conferences with individuals and small groups.

On Sunday FDR proclaimed a national four-day

bank holiday to take effect the next day. This was to stop people from making runs on banks and demanding their savings, which in many instances forced banks to close when they could not meet their depositors' demands. During the bank holiday the economic condition of various banks would be examined, and only those that were sound financially would be allowed to reopen. Those that did reopen would be backed by federal funds to assure their being able to meet all withdrawal demands.

Roosevelt's bank-holiday proclamation also made it illegal to export gold from the country or to demand that currency be redeemed in gold. For months there had been a disastrous drain on the federal gold supply by foreign governments and by American citizens who were hoarding gold and gold certificates (paper money that could be redeemed for actual gold). FDR's proclamation actually took the nation off the gold standard, an act bankers said would end in complete economic collapse. Actually no such thing occurred. Gold began to flow back into the banks in a small trickle, and the value of the dollar in foreign markets was strengthened.

Many people also predicted a disaster during the forced bank holiday, but this fear also proved to be unfounded. The proclamation was greeted in something of a true holiday spirit. The festive mood was caused by a feeling of relief that at long last something was being *done,* no matter how drastic.

When Monday morning dawned and no banks opened their doors, a we're-all-in-this-together mood prevailed. Everybody, of course, was caught with whatever cash they had available. Checks could not be cashed unless the person or business cashing them had a large supply of money on hand, and this was rarely the case. Many businesses, however, did accept checks on faith, trusting that when the banks reopened, the checks would be honored. There were no credit cards in those days, but most hotels adopted a policy of "stay now, pay later." Some hotels in major cities were almost immediately faced with the problem of an influx of patrons from the local skid rows who welcomed the opportunity to spend a few nights in decent lodgings rather than in their usual flophouses.

Most grocery stores sold food on credit. Here and there enterprising newsboys created their own form of scrip—pieces of paper on which two cents or five cents or a similar small sum was written. These they gave to their customers who in turn wrote their names on them and used this makeshift currency to purchase daily newspapers. When real money again became available, this scrip would be redeemed by the newsboys' credit customers. Few ever defaulted. There were also many rumors that the federal government was going to issue scrip in large denominations, but this never came to pass.

In addition to his bank-holiday proclamation, FDR also called an emergency session of Congress. When Congress met on Thursday, March 9, the House passed FDR's Emergency Banking Act in thirty minutes. The Senate took somewhat longer, but the bill was on the President's desk for his signature that same evening. The Emergency Banking Act extended the bank holiday. It also officially authorized a fine of ten thousand dollars for anyone hoarding gold or gold certificates. Gold and gold certificates flooded back into the banks when they reopened.

On Friday, March 10, Roosevelt's second proposed piece of legislation was passed. This was called the Economy Act. It differed from almost every other New Deal measure in that it cut government spending rather than increasing it. There was strong feeling in the business world, however, that part of the nation's ills were being caused by an unbalanced federal budget. In his campaign FDR had promised to balance the budget, and this was his first attempt to do so. The Economy Act cut benefit payments to war veterans as well as the salaries of federal employees. Later these cuts were restored.

All weekend Treasury officials worked to decide which of the nation's nineteen thousand federal and state banks would be allowed to reopen on Monday, March 13. In the end it was decided that twenty-four hundred banks were in sound enough condition to reopen immediately. Most of the others would be allowed to reopen just as soon as they were sufficiently bolstered by federal funds. Some nine hundred, however, were put in the highly doubtful class, and most of these never did reopen. The closing of these banks plus approximately another thousand that eventually failed or merged with stronger banks cost Americans some five billion dollars.

On Sunday evening, March 12, FDR delivered the first of his so-called fireside chats. These were talks delivered over the radio to the American people. They were devised by Roosevelt as a means of remaining close to the American people and explaining to them in clear and simple terms what the New Deal administration had done to date and what it planned to do.

In his first fireside chat, for example, FDR wanted to explain to the people the reasons for the bank holiday and reassure them about the basic soundness of the nation's banks. He pointed out that one of the main reasons for the holiday was to provide money that would meet all demands by depositors when the banks reopened. He spoke in simple, uncomplex terms. In talking about the soundness of the banking system he said, "I can assure you that it is safer to keep your money in a reopened bank than under the mattress."

He went on to say that, for the time being at least, some banks would not reopen without being reorganized. "But," he added, "the new law allows the government to assist in making these reorganizations quickly and effectively and even allows the government to subscribe to at least part of any new capital which may be required."

In conclusion he said, "Confidence and courage are the essentials in carrying out the success of our plan. You people must have faith; you must not be stampeded by rumors or guesses. Let us unite in banishing fear. We have provided the machinery to restore our financial system; it is up to you to support and make it work. It is your problem no less than it is mine. Together we cannot fail."

Some sixty million people listening to twenty million radios that night heard FDR's warm, friendly, supremely confident voice and went to bed and slept better than they had in months.

It had been predicted by some businessmen that when the banks did reopen there would be immediate and disastrous bank runs. But such a panic did not occur. All but nine of New York City's banks reopened on Monday—a pattern that was similar to that in most major cities—and there were indeed long lines of customers before cashiers' windows. But people were depositing more money than they were withdrawing. In New York City alone the Federal Reserve banks reported an excess of ten million dollars at the end of the day, and prices on the New York Stock Exchange increased by more

The New Deal's First Hundred Days

than 15 percent, a spectacular rise reminiscent of the boom days of the twenties.

In Washington FDR and his aides, having won a spectacular victory in this opening battle, returned to the New Deal war against the Depression with renewed enthusiasm.

There was no letup in the rapid rate at which FDR suggested new legislation to Congress and the dispatch with which each new bill was passed. Below are some of the other major bills that were passed during the New Deal's first one hundred days. Several are still among the nation's statutes, and all to some degree changed the course of the country's history.

Civilian Conservation Corps Reforestation Relief Act

The purpose of this bill was to give unemployed young men jobs in healthy surroundings and to help conserve the nation's natural resources. Members of the CCC (or the Three Cs as it was popularly called) were taken off town and city relief rolls, given their room and board, and paid thirty dollars a month. Most of their pay was to be sent home to help support the other members of their needy families. CCC youths worked with the forestry service in improving parks and recreational areas. They also planted trees, built small dams, and erected firebreaks and fire towers. Occasionally they were even called upon to fight forest fires.

Within a few months after the CCC bill was passed, some three hundred thousand youths were living in thirteen hundred old army camps under the direction of United States Army officers. Many of these camps were in the Great Plains area where the CCC planted more than two hundred million trees to eliminate the erosion of topsoil, which had caused severe dust storms and destroyed whole farming regions. Some of the most effective work done by the CCC was in the Great Plains. The creation of the CCC was, in fact, one of the New Deal's most successful measures. When World War II ended this program, more than two and a half million youths had served in the CCC, and they and the nation were vastly improved by their efforts.

Federal Emergency Relief Act

This bill provided an immediate sum of five hundred million dollars for the direct relief of the unemployed. At first this program was administered through state and local agencies, but it was the federal government that provided the funds. Direct relief and job programs for the poor and unemployed eventually grew into the most massive federally funded measures of the New Deal. They were also the largest and most costly in American history. They included the Civil Works Administration (CWA), out of which grew the Works Progress Administration (WPA), and finally a separate and enormous long-range program called the Public Works Administration (PWA). The latter, technically part of the National Recovery Administration, was eventually responsible for helping to build Hoover Dam, New York City's Triborough Bridge, a port at Brownsville, Texas, and the Overseas Highway that led across the Florida keys. PWA funds were also used to build sewage plants in many cities, hospitals, some fifty military airports, and the aircraft carriers *Yorktown* and *Enterprise,* which later helped the United States win World War II.

Agricultural Adjustment Act

The AAA was the New Deal's answer to the farm problem. Crop surpluses were believed to be the main cause of low prices received by the farmers. Crop control would reduce these surpluses. The amount of wheat and corn could be controlled by reducing the number of acres planted in these crops. The farmers were to be paid by the federal government for *not* planting corn and wheat. The 1933 cotton crop, however, was too far advanced, so it was decided to have the cotton farmers plow under much of their crop. Ten million acres of cotton were subsequently plowed under, the farmers receiving two hundred million dollars in benefits for the cotton that was thus kept off the market. To further reduce the use of corn and also reduce the number of hogs going to market (hogs were fed mainly on corn), six million swine were slaughtered for which hog farmers were also paid.

These crop-control measures were widely criticized. Newspapers constantly referred sentimentally to the "slaughter of baby pigs," although nothing was ever said about the normal slaughter of swine for pork in the country's meatpacking houses. In addition, much of the pork from the slaughtered swine was also used for federal food-relief programs, a fact that was seldom reported.

Despite wide criticism, however, the New Deal AAA program was in the beginning highly successful. The price of cotton doubled, and farm prices generally increased to the point where farmers who had been destitute were earning an adequate income. But later in the New Deal, crop control was not nearly as effective, and some of the problems (guaranteeing farmers certain prices for their crops, for example) still exist today. Severe drought in the Great Plains region also eliminated the need for controlling the number of acres planted in corn and wheat.

Tennessee Valley Authority Act

During World War I, a huge hydroelectric power plant had been built by the federal government at Muscle Shoals, Alabama, at a cost of 165 million dollars. Since then, there had been continuous debate about whether this power plant should be privately owned or operated by the government to provide cheap electricity for the general public in the area. Meanwhile, the plant had stood idle. The TVA act put the plant back into operation as a publicly owned facility. The act also provided for the development of the whole Tennessee Valley through the building of other dams and through other federally-funded conservation measures. The Tennessee Valley program soon became famous throughout the world as an example of how a national government could play a positive role in the economic development of a major region. Businessmen in general, however, and public utilities operators in particular objected to this direct move by the federal government. Many regarded it as dangerously socialistic and a threat to the American democratic principle of free enterprise.

National Industrial Recovery Act

One of the basic ideas of this bill was to spread employment by shortening the work week. It was reasoned that if one person normally worked sixty hours a week and his or her work week was cut to thirty hours, this would provide a jobless person with thirty hours of work a week. In addition to establishing a uniform work week of between thirty and forty hours, the NIRA provided a floor under wages so that all workers had to be paid a certain minimum salary. Out of the NIRA grew the National Recovery Administration (NRA). The NRA was an effort to provide the nation with "codes" or agreements that would eliminate "cut-throat competition" in which many businessmen had engaged in an effort to get what little business was available during the Depression. This kind of planned economy was popular in Soviet Russia, and many of the young New Dealers regarded the Soviet Union with great admiration. In the Soviet Union not only prices and wages but also production was strictly regulated by the central government under various so-called Five-Year plans. Some New Dealers hoped eventually to achieve this goal in the United States, with Washington doing all the planning of the nation's economy.

Businesses that operated under the NRA were allowed to display posters in their windows bearing the NRA symbol—an enormous Blue Eagle. Display of these posters was considered a powerful patriotic gesture and an indication that the businessman was doing his part to fight the Depression. The Blue Eagle was in the beginning the most widespread and popular of the New Deal emblems, and the NRA one of the most controversial of the New Deal measures.

Actually the NRA gave FDR and his Democratic administration unprecedented power over American business. Prices could be raised or lowered at will by the President—theoretically to stimulate business when business was bad and put a damper on it when inflation threatened. The NRA, however, was in direct opposition to the nation's Sherman Anti-Trust Act, which made it illegal for major companies to band together and reach certain agreements on wages and prices that could drive smaller companies out of business. The NRA also took away from Congress its law-making powers under the United States Constitution. For these reasons the NRA was eventually declared unconstitutional by the Supreme Court, and the Blue Eagle was allowed to fly away—much to the relief of small businessmen. The controversy and excitement surrounding the NRA, however, did in its own way manage to stimulate the nation into a feeling of renewed optimism about the future of the economy. Once again the people, who had grown weary of economic stagnation, were delighted that at least something was being done.

Banking Act of 1933

This was the final piece of legislation enacted during the New Deal's first hundred days. Its most important feature was the establishment of the Federal Deposit Insurance Corporation (FDIC). The FDIC officially placed a federal guarantee behind deposits in FDIC member banks. When the measure was passed, FDR's critics immediately accused it of being "unsound, unscientific, and dangerous to the economy." Actually the FDIC proved to be just the opposite, as can be judged by the soundness of today's banks. Even in the twenties, bank failures had numbered between three hundred to seven hundred annually. This number soared to an average of more than a thousand a year during the early thirties. Since the passage of the Banking Act of 1933, the average has been about four annually. It is also interesting to note that when the Banking Act was passed and the FDIC was established, individual deposits were insured for amounts up to ten thousand dollars. Today they are fully insured for amounts up to forty thousand dollars.

While all these pieces of legislation were of great interest and importance to the American public, the people behind these measures—FDR and his New Dealers—were certainly of at least equal if not greater interest to the public. FDR, of course, was a constant source of dramatic news. A half-joking, half-serious popular query of the day was "What's that man in the White House going to do next?"

But the men and women around FDR also added their enormous and unique energies to the New Deal whirlwind in Washington. One of the most interesting of these New Dealers was Frances Perkins, the so-called First Lady of the Cabinet who was largely responsible for establishing the Civilian Conservation Corps and other important New Deal measures.

CHAPTER SIX

First Lady of the Cabinet

FRANCES PERKINS often said, "Being a woman has only bothered me in climbing trees."

Long before the days of the women's liberation movement, Frances Perkins had been a leader in the fight for women's rights. And those who had done battle with her knew the fact that she was a woman had never kept her from accomplishing anything she set out to do—and as far as they were concerned, that *included* climbing trees. She was also a fighter for all peoples' rights, especially the rights of the poor—men, women, and children.

Born in Boston in 1882, Frances had known FDR since the early 1900s when he had been a young state senator in Albany, New York. She had been graduated from Mount Holyoke College in Massachusetts in 1902 and shortly afterward became a social worker. She worked for a time with Jane Addams at Hull House, a famous settlement house for the poor, in Chicago, and then took her master's degree in social economics at Columbia University in New York in 1910. She was then named executive secretary of the New York Consumers' League. Her job was to investigate industrial conditions and fight or lobby for legislation to protect working women and children. In her role as a lobbyist, she frequently went to Albany, where the New York legislature met. There she became friendly with FDR.

Women lobbyists were a novelty at that time, and members of the state legislature were somewhat inclined to regard Frances with little respect. But all of them, including FDR, were soon to find out what a fighter she was.

During the winter of 1910 Frances lobbied for a bill to shorten the work week and otherwise improve the working conditions of women and children factory workers. She had little success. Then, in March of 1911, a fire broke out in the ramshackle factory building of the Triangle Shirtwaist Company in New York City. Before the blaze could be put out, almost one hundred and fifty young girls and women had lost their lives.

The Triangle Shirtwaist Company fire became a

torch for industrial reform, and Frances Perkins was among those in the forefront who would not let it die. Major safety reform bills were passed by the state legislature, and the work week was shortened to fifty-four hours. Before that, workers could be forced to work almost any number of hours and under the worst possible conditions. Goading the legislature on to pass these bills was not only Frances Perkins but also the young state senator who had by now become her friend and admirer, Franklin Roosevelt.

From that point on "Madame" Perkins and FDR were inseparable political colleagues. The title of Madame Perkins was given to her by puzzled newspapermen of the day who did not know exactly what to call her when she married Paul C. Wilson in 1913 and announced she would continue to use her maiden name—a virtually unheard-of decision before World War I. In 1916, shortly before the United States entered the conflict, the Wilsons' daughter and only child was born. She was christened Susanna Winslow Perkins Wilson.

During his term as governor of New York, FDR named Frances Perkins the state's industrial commissioner. In this role she further reduced the compulsory work week to forty-eight hours and introduced numerous other important reforms. Although he did not tell her so, FDR had already decided before he became President that if he was elected he would appoint her Secretary of Labor. When he did tell her, she objected, not because a woman had never held the job —nor any other Cabinet post for that matter—but because she was not from the ranks of labor. She insisted that labor and especially American Federation of Labor President William Green would not be politically satisfied with a Secretary of Labor who was an outsider. But FDR insisted that she was the right person for the job, and she finally accepted.

Frances Perkins wasted little time in going to work after FDR's inauguration. And soon Madame Perkins, an aggressive, talkative, yet somehow pleasant little woman, began to make almost as much news as her boss, the President himself. She was a highly visible New Dealer, not only because she was the only woman in an otherwise all-male Cabinet but also because she always wore a three-cornered hat called a tricorn. The tricorn had been her badge of office back almost as far as she or anyone else could remember.

Secretary Perkins' first major effort had to do with the Civilian Conservation Corps. It was her pet New Deal project. In one of her early interviews with the press she explained how the program was started:

"When the President and the Cabinet first got together to make plans for immediate work relief," she said, "all of the emphasis was placed on providing jobs for men who were out of work. While I heartily approved these measures,

First Lady of the Cabinet

I asked President Roosevelt not to forget about the millions of boys and young men who were also out of work.

"I pointed out that a number of these youngsters have become migrants. They're riding freight trains from one part of the country to another in a desperate search for jobs. In fact my Department's Children's Bureau has already reported that several hundred thousand boys, and girls dressed as boys, are drifting around the country as hoboes. It's a deplorable situation. The President agreed that it is.

" 'How do you propose to remedy the situation?' he asked me.

"I said I thought camps should be set up for unemployed boys and young men, camps where the boys can do such things as forestry work.

"Mr. Roosevelt again agreed. 'How do you think the boys can be selected and processed?' he asked me.

" 'That's what's been puzzling me,' I said. 'I think the camps themselves could be staffed by Army men—but the training would not be military training.'

"President Roosevelt reminded me that when he and I first talked about my taking the Secretary of Labor job, I mentioned wanting to establish a Federal Employment Service similar to the New York State Employment Service. 'Why not do that now?' he asked me, 'and have the Federal Employment Service process the men?'

"I told him I hadn't done anything about establishing such a service yet.

" 'Then establish it,' President Roosevelt said.

"And that's what I'm in the process of doing. The Federal or United States Employment Service will soon be ready to select and process boys for the CCC just as soon as Congress passes the legislation."

"How much will each CCC member be paid?" a newspaperman asked.

"Each boy must come from a family on relief, and he will be paid a dollar a day for his work. All of the costs for his board, lodging, clothes, education, and medical care will be met by the government. He will send all of what he earns except for twenty-five cents a week to his family, and the family relief allowance will be reduced by that amount."

"How do you think William Green is going to react to this plan?" another reporter asked.

"He's already reacted," Frances Perkins said. "He was horrified by the idea of establishing a dollar a day as the wage for any work. I've tried to explain to him that this is relief money, not a wage scale. 'Just the same,' Mr. Green told me, 'the boys will be getting it as wages.' I told him it was just being called wages to save face, to give the boys a little pride in earning some money by the sweat of their brows."

"How does the President feel about Mr. Green's reaction?"

"He's disappointed. He thought labor would be delighted with the CCC."

Frances Perkins had been right about William Green. As soon as her appointment to the Cabinet was announced, Green declared that he and the rest of organized labor would never become reconciled to it. Eventually, however, he came around and became one of the staunch supporters of the CCC as well as other projects. Part of Green's about-face was due to the fact that it was Secretary Perkins who insisted that the New Deal legislation include a minimum wage for all workers.

The CCC proved to be an instant success. The Labor Department's Employment Service selected and processed the men. Army officers and noncommissioned officers were in charge of the camps, and the Forestry Service supervised the daily work. When it began, the CCC enlisted boys and young men in their teens. Later, older men were admitted. The program was so successful that it led to several individual states establishing similar camps for dependent, delinquent, or neglected young people.

In later years, after she had retired as Secretary of Labor, Frances Perkins was frequently stopped by men who would say to her, "You were a friend of FDR's. He must have been a great guy. I was in the Three Cs, and it was the best experience I ever had in my life."

One of the reasons the several million veterans of the Three Cs were so enthusiastic about their experience was because it went far beyond its original purpose of providing constructive work and relief from poverty. It was FDR who stressed the CCC's "moral and spiritual values." It was he who insisted that the corps should also have an educational and rehabilitation program. Many of the young men were not only jobless but also poorly educated and physically below par. CCC instructors and medical advisers were assigned to the various camps to remedy this. Almost without exception, members were instilled with new confidence and a desire and ability to go back to work in their hometowns and cities.

Originally certain charges were made against the CCC; it was claimed that the organization was militaristic, that the camps were a camouflage behind which active military training was being carried on. In Germany the Adolf Hitler regime was busy creating youth camps and labor battalions that engaged in poorly disguised military training for boys and young men. It was feared that this was also the real purpose of the CCC. Actually nothing could have been further from the truth.

The army officers in charge of the camps were under strict orders to impose absolutely no military training on the young men. In addition the officers had no control over the youths during the day while they were at work. Park or forestry or soil-erosion supervisors were in charge of all jobs, and it was their influence that was felt most strongly in the camps. All in all, the CCC through its combination of work, education, and physical rehabilitation reached poor, underprivileged young men as nothing else in their lives had been able to do up to that time.

And as far as some secret desire on the part of the army to use the CCC for military purposes was concerned, quite the opposite was the case. Many regular army officers objected strongly to being assigned to CCC duty which put them in charge of civilians over whom they were unable to exert any military authority. In the end, however, they, too, changed their opinions after having undergone the experience. One of them later told Frances Perkins, "The Three Cs gave me the greatest course in leadership I ever had. It taught me the importance of controlling and leading men by persuasion and example rather than by iron-fisted authority. Later when we got into World War II and disciplinary problems came up, we had already learned how to solve them by persuasion and diplomacy."

As soon as she was certain that the CCC was on the road to success, Frances Perkins turned her attention to other legislation that would improve the welfare of the entire nation—not just a segment of it as was the case with the Three Cs. One of these pieces of legislation was the Social Security Act, a measure whose benefits—and problems—are still with us today. Meanwhile, of course, FDR and his other aides and Cabinet members were hard at work on equally dramatic New Deal measures.

President Franklin D. Roosevelt

FDR as a boy of ten

FDR and his wife, Eleanor, with their children in 1916

The farmer who owned this home in Arkansas was stricken with economic hard times.

Unemployed men line up for a free meal at a soup kitchen.

FDR's first presidential cabinet. Seated, from left to right: George H. Dern, Secretary of War; Cordell Hull, Secretary of State; Franklin D. Roosevelt; William H. Woodin, Secretary of the Treasury; and Homer S. Cummings, Attorney General. Standing, from left to right: Henry A. Wallace, Secretary of Agriculture; Harold L. Ickes, Secretary of the Interior; Claude A. Swanson, Secretary of the Navy; James A. Farley, Postmaster General; Daniel C. Roper, Secretary of Commerce; and Frances Perkins, Secretary of Labor.   ASSOCIATED PRESS PHOTO

ASSOCIATED PRESS PHOTO

ASSOCIATED PRESS PHOTO

Clockwise from top left: *General Hugh "Ironpants" Johnson, FDR and Harry Hopkins, FDR and Henry Wallace, Harold L. Ickes, and Frances Perkins.*

ASSOCIATED PRESS PHOTO

WIDE WORLD PHOTOS

ASSOCIATED PRESS PHOTO

FRANKLIN D. ROOSEVELT LIBRARY

Opposite: *CCC boys fighting a fire*

Below: *FDR on a visit to a CCC camp at Big Meadows, Virginia. Also in the picture are FDR's secretary and close aide Louis Howe and Secretary of the Interior Harold Ickes (seated second and third from the left). Secretary of Agriculture Henry Wallace and Resettlement Administrator Rexford Tugwell are seated at the right.*

FRANKLIN D. ROOSEVELT LIBRARY

Eleanor and Franklin Roosevelt in Washington with their grandchildren

FRANKLIN D. ROOSEVELT LIBRARY

The Little White House at Warm Springs, Georgia

FRANKLIN D. ROOSEVELT WARM SPRINGS MEMORIAL COMMISSION

CHAPTER SEVEN

Felix Frankfurter's Happy Hot Dogs

TWO OF THE MOST controversial New Deal agencies were set up to help both the nation's poverty-stricken farmers and city workers. They were the Agricultural Adjustment Administration (AAA) and the National Recovery Administration (NRA). The AAA and NRA were headed by several men who were also among the most colorful and controversial of all the New Dealers. Secretary and Assistant Secretary of Agriculture Henry A. Wallace and Rexford G. Tugwell headed the AAA, and General Hugh "Ironpants" Johnson the NRA. Frances Perkins also had a hand in early NRA activity, but even the aggressive and colorful Madame Perkins could not steal any of the limelight from Ironpants Johnson. The NRA, while it lasted, was always a one-man show, and Johnson was it.

In 1935 and 1936 the NRA and AAA respectively were declared unconstitutional, but before then they stirred up a storm of activity and controversy the like of which the nation's capital and the nation itself had seldom seen.

Henry Agard Wallace was both a practical man and an idealistic dreamer. An Iowa farmboy, he had gone to work on the staff of the family magazine, *Wallace's Farmer,* after graduating from Iowa State College at Ames in 1910. When his father became Secretary of Agriculture under President Harding, young Wallace took over the editorship of the magazine.

Wallace's practical side was shown in his experiments with hybrid seed corn that led to the development of a variety of corn that had enormous yields of grain per acre. His idealistic, even mystic side was shown in his belief that through total government planning and crop control the nation need never suffer from either crop shortages or surpluses. This idea he called "the ever-normal granary."

Wallace was brought to FDR's attention by Rexford Tugwell. As an economics professor at Columbia University, Tugwell had read a number of Wallace's articles on agricultural economy in *Wallace's Farmer* and thought the Iowan's ideas fitted in with FDR's New Deal philosophy. FDR and his top aide at that time, Raymond Moley, agreed.

Tugwell, like Wallace, also believed in government

planning and control of the nation's farm economy. At Columbia he had taught this theory and had written several books and articles on the subject. Born in upstate New York, Tugwell had been a teacher all his adult life and thus had had none of Wallace's practical farm experience. Nonetheless, he was eager to put his theories into practice. Together the two men went to work to rescue the nation's farmers.

They were aided in their work by a group of enormously enthusiastic young aides known throughout Washington as "Felix Frankfurter's Happy Hot Dogs." Felix Frankfurter was a professor in the Harvard University Law School and a long-time friend and adviser of FDR. When FDR was selecting the members of his Cabinet, he had seriously considered Frankfurter for some top role, but the Harvard professor respectfully declined. He was, however, a great admirer of FDR and the New Deal and spent much time and effort in recruiting bright young men to fill many of the key administrative jobs in Washington.

Most of the Happy Hot Dogs who swarmed into Washington—literally by the hundreds—were young lawyers or teachers. They were attracted by FDR himself and the New Deal challenge. Many felt they were on a mission to save the republic from disaster. Eagerly they took jobs in all of the New Deal agencies, working endless hours, partying with equal enthusiasm, and spouting a steady stream of ideas in their passionate crusade for the return of prosperity. Many of them held relatively anonymous yet highly important positions under Frances Perkins, Wallace, Tugwell, and Ironpants Johnson, as well as serving as aides in the White House, Congress, and elsewhere in the Roosevelt administration.

The destruction of crops and the killing of pigs and brood sows to create an economy of scarcity and thus raise farm prices were not undertaken lightly by Henry Wallace and his aides. As a former farmer, Wallace regarded these acts as unfortunate but necessary. The farm economy was in a state of crisis and had been since the 1920s. Something drastic simply had to be done. The reduction of the number of acres farmers could plant in crops was, however, regarded with more enthusiasm by Wallace since it fitted in with his idea about an ever-normal granary.

Payment to the farmers, both for crop and animal destruction and for the acres they kept out of production, was to be made through a so-called processing tax. This tax was levied on millers, meat packers, and others who processed and distributed farm products. Farmers were not forced to join the program of keeping part of their land out of production, called acreage allotment, but those who did not would not receive any federal aid from this processing tax. Consequently, most farmers joined the program.

Many critics violently opposed the AAA program.

They claimed the destruction of animals and crops was an evil act, one that was against the laws of God and man. The acreage-allotment plan, they insisted, was even worse. Not only was it unnatural and immoral, but it smacked of Communist Russia's undemocratic planned economy. Both Wallace and Tugwell were accused by many conservatives of "selling out to Russia."

Nevertheless, within a matter of months after it went into effect, the new farm program showed marked signs of success. Farm incomes were up; farm debt was reduced; and surpluses were much lower than they had been in years. This silenced some critics but not all. They pointed out that the reduction in surpluses was not due solely to the program itself. Much of the reduction was also due to drought and the fact that many farms were being blown away by windstorms in the dust-bowl states of Oklahoma, the Dakotas, and others in the Great Plains region.

The dust-bowl drama was one of the great tragedies of the Depression era. Poor farming methods, which had destroyed the protective sod that had once covered the topsoil of the Great Plains, plus periods of drought, and finally great windstorms had resulted in the destruction of whole farming regions. Until effective soil-conservation measures could be taken by the Agriculture Department, the CCC, and other agencies, as well as by farmers themselves, much of the Great

Plains would be useless for crops and totally unlivable.

Dust storms in the Great Plains states turned night into day. The great dark clouds of sandlike topsoil were carried so high into the air over the Dakotas and dispersed over such a wide area that they affected the atmosphere as far away as the eastern seaboard. People moved out of the dust bowl by the tens of thousands. Many moved into the already economically overburdened cities, but many others—especially those from Arkansas and Oklahoma, who were called Arkies and Okies—migrated to places as far away as California. It was out of this migration to the promised land of the Far West that John Steinbeck's epic novel, *The Grapes of Wrath,* was born.

Until nature and conservation plans could come to their aid, the dispossessed farmers of the Midwest and Southwest had to be cared for by direct federal aid. This aid was in the form of money dispensed by the Federal Relief Administration under Harry Hopkins. In addition, destitute farm families were aided by an agency called the Resettlement Administration under Rexford Tugwell. This agency, created at the direct request of FDR, granted farmers loans to begin farming again in areas where the soil was good and the weather more favorable than in the dust bowl. It also helped establish people in small business enterprises, such as handcraft work and the like.

The Resettlement Administration was most effective in the cotton- and tobacco-growing regions of the South and Southwest and in the mining areas of the Appalachian Mountain region. Here dispossessed sharecroppers and out-of-work miners were literally starving to death, until they were relocated in more fertile regions or subsidized in undertaking small business ventures, making quilts, bedspreads, and clothing. FDR's wife, Eleanor Roosevelt, took a keen interest in this program, and worked closely with Tugwell and his Happy Hot Dog aides on it, especially in the Appalachian region. To many Appalachian families Eleanor Roosevelt, who often visited and worked among them, *was* the New Deal, and they never forgot her.

Meanwhile, the severe plight of city workers and businessmen had to be dealt with also. An economic situation that had already been desperate was made even worse by the influx of migrating farm workers into urban areas. The immediate needs of city dwellers were met by direct relief funds, but all the New Dealers from FDR and his Brain Trust on down through the bright young Happy Hot Dogs agreed that the only solution was to create new jobs by getting business back on its feet. This task fell to Ironpants Johnson and the NRA.

Hugh S. Johnson was born at Fort Scott, Kansas, and was graduated from West Point in 1903 in the same class with Douglas MacArthur. Johnson's hard-riding, hell-for-leather early career as a young cavalryman serving with the United States Army in Mexico in 1916 earned him the Ironpants nickname. During World War I he was in charge of the draft, or selective service system, attaining the rank of brigadier general. He also served on the War Industries Board under financier Bernard Baruch. This board organized American business to help in the war effort and probably gave Johnson the idea for his NRA plan of organizing business to fight a war against the Depression.

After World War I, Johnson entered the business world himself at the urging of Baruch, for whom he acted as an economics adviser. An extremely versatile man, Johnson had a rough, tough exterior which concealed a wide-ranging knowledge of business, law, economics, agriculture, and even literature and folklore. His interest in literature led to his writing several excellent books for boys. Raymond Moley regarded Johnson as a genius.

Genius or not, Johnson was difficult. He did not work well with others, preferring to dream up dramatic ideas and then see them through to completion himself. He occasionally drank to excess and would sometimes disappear for days at a time at crucial periods. He also had a violent temper with a profane vocabulary to match—doubtless, a carry-over from his cavalry days.

Nevertheless, Johnson was a person with inspired ideas, and this was the thing that appealed to FDR. One of his most inspired ideas was the NRA. FDR believed it would dramatize the whole New Deal program, and drama was what the Depression-dazed public needed.

The NRA was supposed to do for city workers what the AAA was doing for the farmers—increase their income through an increased number of jobs created by new and revived business and manufacturing. Johnson believed this could only be accomplished by a government-planned economy. FDR and the Brain Trust agreed.

American business had operated for years in an independent fashion that bordered on anarchy. American businessmen could do virtually anything they pleased to make money. Their sense of responsibility to the people who worked for them, and toward each other, was almost nonexistent.

In the past there had been various efforts to curb business anarchy. These efforts included the passage of antitrust laws and in 1914 the establishment of a Federal Trade Commission. Generally speaking, however, businessmen had fought against any and all government control, even that which was aimed at ending destructive competition—big businesses gobbling up little ones and thus throwing people out of work. But the Depression had so badly damaged all business—between 1929 and 1933 it had been cut in half—that businessmen pleaded with FDR for any action that would lead to recovery.

Johnson's plan was to create federally licensed trade associations within which the various types of business would operate—a Building Trades' Association, an Automobile Manufacturers' Association, a Coal Operators' Association, and so on. The government, working with the heads of the various associations, would decide the amount of goods to be produced, the price at which goods could be sold, and the wages paid to workers.

It was Frances Perkins who insisted upon a forty-hour work week at a specific wage level. She was also influential in making collective bargaining legal, which meant that certain demands of employee's unions could now be negotiated. This led to the powerful role that labor unions have played in the nation's economy ever since the NRA.

As it was finally passed by Congress, the NRA legislation also included a provision for codes of conduct that each of the trade associations within the NRA would agree to follow. But there were no penalties for noncompliance with the codes of conduct. FDR had insisted such penalties were necessary if the NRA was to work, but Congress disagreed. This was a fatal flaw.

Since membership in the NRA trade associations was purely voluntary and there were no penalties for those who joined and failed to live up to the codes of conduct, the entire program became one in which businessmen were merely on their honor to comply.

Dishonest businessmen and small-time chiselers finally wrecked the NRA months before it was declared unconstitutional. One of the ways they did so was to agree that they would hire the same number of workers and pay them the same wages as their competitors, turn out so much of a specific product, and sell it at a certain price. Then while their competitors followed the code of conduct for their particular trade association, they themselves hired as few people as possible as cheaply as possible, to turn out as much as they could at a sure profit. In addition, big businesses made a point of creating codes of conduct that would force small businesses out of existence. Thus the same old destructive competition was in effect.

Despite these inherent flaws in the NRA legislation, Ironpants Johnson set about making the program work. He did so with all the zeal of an evangelist or crusader. He actually told newsmen that he thought the NRA was a holy thing. Johnson always insisted the NRA could only work on a voluntary basis anyway, so the lack of penalties didn't actually make any difference. And for a time the NRA did seem to work. Most of the public and business leaders as well flocked to follow the NRA symbol, the big Blue Eagle banner, as eagerly as they had flocked to follow the national colors in America's past wars.

Johnson was an excellent showman. Since he believed the success or failure of the NRA would be a matter of mass psychology, he attempted to court success with a kind of Blue Eagle mass hysteria that was similar to the war-bond drives of World War I. Millions of Blue Eagle banners were distributed throughout the United States. The symbol appeared in every store and factory window and was also printed on grocery products and packages, clothing, automobiles, and almost everything else that was manufactured and sold. Cities held Blue Eagle days featuring parades in which marchers carried Blue Eagle banners. "We Do Our Part" was the NRA slogan, and it too appeared virtually everywhere—even on men's neckties and on women's scarves.

For a time business did show definite signs of recovery as a result of the onslaught of NRA propaganda. Unemployment went down and the stock market went up and General Ironpants Johnson seemed to be the business savior he was claimed to be. But gradually the fatal flaws began to appear, and the old fighting and bickering and cheating among the nation's businessmen began once again. Soon the Blue Eagle became something of a national joke, and it began to disappear from store and factory windows and other displays as quickly as it had appeared—but with much less fanfare.

Johnson himself became more than discouraged when employment failed to increase by the six million he had predicted by Labor Day of 1933. FDR, too, became disillusioned and made no effort to keep Johnson on the job when he offered to resign the following year. FDR was still personally fond of Johnson, but by nature the President was not a person to continue following a losing cause and he had concluded that the NRA was just that. Roosevelt had often said that the New Deal would try many things: some would work, and some would not. Those that did not would be abandoned. The NRA was abandoned. And following FDR's lead, the mercurial Happy Hot Dogs quickly looked about them for other New Deal causes to champion.

Johnson left office in the fall of 1934, and the NRA was declared unconstitutional the following spring because it broke the nation's fair trade and antitrust laws. FDR made no effort to revive it in a new more legally acceptable form. In discussing its death with Frances Perkins, FDR said, "We've gotten the best out of the NRA anyway. Industry got a shot in the arm. Everything has started up again. I don't believe they'll go back to the old wage and work levels. I think the forty-hour week will stick except for a few instances. I think the NRA has perhaps done all it can."

But FDR was not so calm in January 1936, when the Supreme Court declared the AAA was also unconstitutional. The tax on those who processed farmers' products was illegal, the Supreme Court said, because it eliminated free enterprise by discriminating against the processors. They were being forced to pay a tax so that the farmers would make money, but the tax was driving many of the processors into bankruptcy. This was discriminatory and unfair and thus unconstitutional, the Supreme Court said.

The declaration that the AAA was unconstitutional was a severe blow to both the farmers, who were still very much in favor of it, and to FDR and his New Deal. By this time—early 1936—both farm prices and farmers' incomes had risen by about 60 percent. Consequently, FDR directed Wallace and Tugwell and their young aides to see what they could do about preparing an alternative plan. This they did in very short order.

The new legislation was ingenious, and, under tremendous pressure from the farm belt, Congress quickly passed it. Farmers were paid to keep cropland out of production, but not—and this was the ingenious device—to keep down surpluses, except for conservation purposes. Continued soil erosion could be stopped, Wallace insisted, by allowing land to go unplowed, thus allowing the protective grass and sod cover to take hold. The processing tax was eliminated, and farmers were paid from funds appropriated by Congress for soil-conservation purposes. This plan, modified somewhat in 1938 to include specific details for Wallace's ever-normal granary, was quite similar to the agricultural program that is still in effect today. Under it, moderate surpluses of staple crops are bought and stored by the government as reserves to meet crop failures in bad years.

CHAPTER EIGHT

Hunger Is Not Debatable

"PEOPLE DON'T EAT in the long run, son. They eat every day"—that was what Harry Hopkins told one of his young Happy Hot Dog aides who had proposed a complicated relief program that he was sure "would work out in the long run."

"The unemployed are hungry *now,*" Hopkins went on, "and long-range plans aren't going to fill their bellies tomorrow or pay their overdue rent bills."

FDR appointed the outspoken Harry Hopkins head of the Federal Emergency Relief Administration on May 12, 1933, the day Congress created the agency. By the end of that same day Hopkins had given away five million of the five hundred million dollars in relief funds appropriated by Congress to get the agency under way. It did not take Hopkins long to give away the rest and come back to Congress asking for millions more.

When cautioned that the House Appropriations Committee might have to debate the need for such huge additional funds, Hopkins snapped, "Hunger is not debatable."

Privately Hopkins told Frances Perkins, "I only expect to be in this job for six months before they throw me out so I might as well do as much good as I can for the poor and hungry as fast as I can."

Hopkins was wrong about the length of his term of service. He was to serve FDR, FDR's successor Harry Truman, and the nation until the end of World War II. He was not wrong, however, about the millions of people whom he helped to live better lives, or the aid he gave the nation in moving toward economic recovery.

Harry Hopkins had been familiar with poverty from the time he was a boy growing up in the Midwest. Born in Sioux City, Iowa, in 1890, he was the fourth child in a family of five. His father was an unsuccessful traveling harness salesman who finally settled in Grinnell, Iowa, where he operated a combination harness shop and school store that supplied candy, newspapers, magazines, and school supplies to the students attending Grinnell College. The Hopkins family never had enough money, but young Harry did manage to work his way through Grinnell College, where he was an average student, an excellent athlete, and an outstanding campus politician.

Partly inspired by his mother, who was an extremely religious woman, and also guided by several college professors, young Harry went into social-welfare work immediately after his graduation. His first job as a social worker was at Christadora House, a settlement house in the middle of New York City's East Side slums. There he worked with boys' clubs in an environment of human misery—flophouses, tenement dwellings, and sweatshops where men, women, and children worked long hours for a few pennies a day. Hopkins himself earned only a few dollars a week. He never forgot the misery he encountered in New York's slums, and he vowed to spend the rest of his life, if necessary, fighting against such conditions. The Depression and FDR's New Deal gave him his golden opportunity.

As a welfare worker in New York, Hopkins had become close friends with both Frances Perkins and FDR. As governor, Roosevelt had appointed him director of New York's Temporary Emergency Relief Administration. Hopkins was in that job when FDR became President and put him in charge of the New Deal emergency relief program.

FDR had come to know and respect Hopkins as a

completely loyal and selfless man. When asked one time why he kept on as his close aide such an outspoken and controversial figure as Harry Hopkins, FDR said, "If you were ever to become President, you would be looking through that door and knowing that practically everybody who walked through it wanted something from you. You would learn what a lonely job this is, and you would discover the need for somebody like Harry Hopkins, who asks for nothing except to serve you."

The New Deal relief program was actually split into two parts. One dealt with immediate emergency relief, the other with long-range goals. Hopkins headed the first part of the program. The second part was headed by Harold Ickes in his Cabinet role as Secretary of the Interior. There soon developed a bitter feud between them.

Ickes was every bit as headstrong and outspoken as Hopkins. He proudly called himself "the Old Curmudgeon," a term that meant he was a cross, ill-tempered, bad-natured, stubborn old man. Most people agreed that Ickes had chosen the term wisely. He was also, however, called "Honest Harold" because, friend and foe alike agreed, he was a completely honest public servant as well as a shrewd and skilled administrator.

Born of Dutch ancestry in Blair Country, Pennsylvania, in 1874, Ickes was a graduate of the University of Chicago Law School. He then practiced law, worked as a newspaper columnist, and became active in politics. He was originally a Republican, but his liberal leanings led him into the Progressive party under Teddy Roosevelt and Wisconsin Senator Robert LaFollette, and then into the Democratic party under FDR.

Hopkins and Ickes had their first serious clash over the New Deal's work relief program. The winter of 1933–34 was one of the most bitterly cold winters in American history. The severe weather combined with massive unemployment to create a situation of tremendous hardship and misery. Hopkins proposed to deal with the situation immediately; Ickes continued with long-range plans.

Under Ickes and the Department of the Interior, the Public Works Administration (PWA) had set in motion many major projects that included the building of bridges and dams, the construction of highways, and the improvement of the nation's railway system. Eventually such public works would employ many thousands of men. But to Hopkins "eventually" was not now, and Ickes' plans smacked too much of the old Republican "trickle-down" theory. Hopkins favored what he called a "trickle-up" theory—putting money immediately into the hands of the poor, who would spend it and thus put other people to work providing goods and services.

Hopkins suggested to FDR that at least four million men be put to work immediately, but on a short-term basis—just through the winter months. The work created for the unemployed would include local projects in their own communities—repairing roads and streets, improving parks, digging ditches, remodeling and repairing schools and other public buildings, working as office helpers and researchers, and teaching those who could not read or were completely unskilled.

FDR liked Hopkins' plan and decided to take the money needed for it from Ickes' PWA funds. Within a week—despite Ickes' protests over the siphoning off of his agency's money—FDR had issued an executive order establishing the Civil Works Administration (CWA). Local authorities were, of course, enormously pleased with the CWA, but no more pleased than the unemployed who now found themselves back at work, even though the jobs were makeshift, with money in their pockets. To FDR and Hopkins the most important thing of all was the fact that people who had been out of work for months and years were now regaining their self-respect.

But Ickes, along with a number of other critics, regarded the CWA as a gigantic "boondoggle" and CWA workers "a bunch of leaf-rakers and shovel-leaners." The term *boondoggle* is said to have been coined in 1925 by Robert H. Link, a Boy Scout leader from

Rochester, New York, who used it to describe a handmade neckerchief slide. Link may have gotten the word from an earlier day, however, since pioneers were also said to have used it to describe certain kinds of handcraft. During the New Deal era it came to be applied to any unnecessary or wasteful project. Tugwell claimed that Ironpants Johnson first used the term in criticizing Hopkins' program after resigning as NRA director.

Nevertheless, the CWA took hold and by mid-January 1934 almost four and a half million men had been put back to work and were in turn putting the money they earned back into the nation's economy. So successful was this pump-priming program in fact that, when it was scheduled to end in the spring of 1934, FDR requested and received additional funds from Congress to keep it going. Later, with all of those on the CWA rolls again threatened with having to go back on direct relief, FDR decided the work relief program should be continued under a new and more permanent agency—the Works Progress Administration (WPA). To this end he requested from Congress an appropriation of almost five billion dollars, at least a part of which was to go to Ickes' long-range public works program. Despite the staggering size of the requested appropriation, Congress passed the bill on March 23, 1935, by a large majority. Immediately Hopkins and Ickes began to struggle for a major share of this vast sum. When open warfare between the two men and their aides threatened, FDR called the two sides together for a peace meeting at his family home in Hyde Park, New York.

Both sides wrangled all day over the allocation of the funds and who should administer the program. In the end it was decided Hopkins would be director of the WPA, which would get the lion's share of the funds, Ickes and the PWA getting only five hundred million dollars. Ickes seriously considered resigning but was talked out of it by FDR. Hopkins, on the other hand, according to Ickes' diary, "acted like he had come out top dog and he meant to keep it that way."

The WPA was actually an expansion of the CWA. Its immediate goal was not only to put four million unemployed back to work but also to keep them at work—and off the direct relief rolls. Workers were paid between fifty and sixty dollars a month. This was considered a livable wage in most communities at the time. Between 1935 and 1939, ten billion dollars was spent on projects that employed between two and four million people a year. Ten percent of the overall sum was paid by local communities, the rest by the federal government. Occasionally some state or city would fail to come up with their 10 percent in matching funds, and then Hopkins would have to threaten them with a complete cutoff in all funds. This invariably brought results.

In all, more than ten million people worked on WPA projects that included the old CWA "made work," such as leaf raking and ditch digging, and also the construction of airports, school buildings, parks, roads, streets, bridges, and even entire sewage systems. In rural areas thousands of new outhouses were also built, a project that caused much sarcastic comment in the media of the day, but one that was important to the health and welfare of many communities. Several major WPA projects included the construction of New York's La Guardia Field, the improvement of the Mississippi River waterfront in St. Louis and other river port cities, and the salvaging of the entire municipal government of Key West, Florida. Key West had gone bankrupt, and before the WPA came to its rescue it was turning into a decaying, abandoned city. Numerous other towns and cities also received major rehabilitation through the WPA.

Out-of-work educators were hired to teach illiterates in ghetto areas and to work as teacher and library aides. Also in the education field, a division of the WPA called the National Youth Administration (NYA) helped young people complete their schooling. Part-time jobs were created by the NYA in high schools and colleges. These jobs included work as clerks and typists, as well as assistants in public-relations offices, libraries, laboratories, campus maintenance, and in various classroom roles, including that of instructor.

NYA pay was not high—high school students earned six dollars a month, college students up to twenty dollars a month, and graduate students up to thirty dollars—but to many students it meant they could stay in school rather than drop out.

In all, the NYA gave part-time employment to six hundred thousand college students and one and a half million high school students. Some two and a half million jobless youths between the ages of sixteen and twenty-four who were not in school were also aided by the NYA. For these young people, who for one reason or another could not join the CCC but whose families were on relief, light construction work similar to the WPA jobs for older people was provided at a wage of between twenty and thirty dollars a month.

Partly due to the NYA program, college enrollments greatly increased between 1935 and the start of World War II. An interesting fact is that the state director for the NYA program in Texas was later to be President of the United States—Lyndon Baines Johnson.

Among the best-known WPA programs were those that gave employment to out-of-work artists and writers. Between 1935 and 1939 the Federal Writers' Project aided six thousand unemployed writers. Among those who later went on to great success were John Cheever, Richard Wright, and Nelson Algren. The Writers' Project produced four hundred books that were published commercially, including fifty-one state and territorial guides in the American Guide series. Many of these have been revised and are still in print today. Richard Wright, famous black author of *Native Son,* worked on this series as well as on a WPA guide to Harlem.

The Federal Art Project, which put artists to work in such jobs as decorating the nation's post offices with murals, employed such future artistic greats as William de Kooning, Thomas Hart Benton, and Jackson Pollock.

The Federal Theater Project was equally important. Not only did it give work to actors, directors, designers, and others, it also brought the theater to many people in rural communities who had never before seen live acting. A Federal Music Project employed hundreds of out-of-work musicians in city symphonies, as well as in local community civic orchestras, some of which are still active today.

All in all, Harry Hopkins' Works Progress Administration—supported by Harold Ickes' Public Works Administration in a secondary yet highly important role—proved to be the most revolutionary as well as one of the most successful of the New Deal measures. Its influence lingered until well after World War II, when the WPA was abolished, in such measures as the Job Corps program and other federally funded poverty relief programs of the 1960s and 1970s.

CHAPTER NINE

End of the New Deal Honeymoon

ACTUALLY THE NEW DEAL honeymoon came to a close somewhere between the end of the First Hundred Days and the end of FDR's first year in office. Millions of people who had been out of work now had jobs, but major unemployment continued to be a problem. This caused many of the long-suffering poor to listen to false prophets preaching crackpot panaceas and to take part in foolish schemes to eliminate poverty. In a curious way these schemes were eventually responsible for the passage of America's first Social Security Act.

One of the odd-ball schemes in which Americans took part was the chain-letter craze. So far as is known this started in Denver, Colorado, in 1934. A person would receive a letter with a dozen or more names listed in it. The recipient was supposed to send a dime to the top name on the list, scratch out that name, add his or her name to the bottom of the list, and then forward copies of the letter to a dozen or more new people. To break the chain was supposed to be bad luck. But, theoretically, if one did not break the chain hundreds of send-a-dime letters would soon fill one's mailbox. This never happened, of course, since the chain was always broken and the only one to profit, if anybody did, was the schemer who had sent out the letter in the first place. Today such chain letters are illegal—they were declared illegal soon after they began to flood the mails—but in 1934 and 1935 literally hundreds of thousands of people took part in them.

The Denver post office alone was flooded with 160,000 chain letters a day, requiring postal workers to put in some twenty-eight thousand hours of overtime during the height of the chain-letter craze. Soon send-a-dime chains were operating in Omaha, Kansas City, Chicago, Los Angeles, Spokane, Topeka, and New York City. In Springfield, Missouri, a chain-letter factory was set up that made eighteen thousand dollars in the few days it was allowed to operate. In many cities office workers spent much of their working day cranking out such letters. In those days, of course,

End of the New Deal Honeymoon

there were no instant copying machines such as are available today, so carbon copies of letters had to be made and occasionally mimeograph machines were used. Even FDR received several thousand chain letters in the White House. He did not hesitate to break the chain, but the fact that Americans could be duped into taking part in such nonsense made him realize more than ever the desperate straits the nation was in.

When chain letters were declared illegal, some schemers sent five-dollar and ten-dollar chain telegrams before these, too, were declared illegal. Others, such as the members of the Liquid Assets Club at Lincoln, Nebraska, resorted to send-a-pint-of-whiskey letters. Theoretically, a person who did not break the chain would eventually receive more than fifteen thousand pints of whiskey.

As suddenly and as mysteriously as it began, the chain-letter craze ended. But there were numerous other equally unsound schemes that much of the public took even more seriously.

For example, in 1933, a man named Upton Sinclair proposed a program on the West Coast which he called "End Poverty in California" (EPIC). Since California had a higher proportion of old people than other states, one feature of EPIC had an especially strong appeal. This was Sinclair's plan to give every unemployed person over sixty a monthly pension of fifty dollars. Sinclair never made clear exactly where this money was to come from.

In 1926 Sinclair had run unsuccessfully for governor of California on the Socialist ticket. In 1933 he was again planning on running for governor, this time as a Democrat, and he believed that his program to end poverty in California would get him elected. In addition to pensions for unemployed old people, EPIC included proposals to increase income and inheritance taxes, to tax idle land, and to establish a statewide system of cooperative business ventures that would stimulate the economy. Sinclair lost the election in 1934 by the narrowest of margins. After his defeat, EPIC collapsed.

Another California-based end-poverty movement was Dr. Francis E. Townsend's "Old Age Revolving Pensions." The Townsend Plan proposed to pay all unemployed persons over sixty years of age two hundred dollars a month. This money had to be spent within thirty days. Funds to support the Townsend Plan were to be obtained through a 2 percent transaction tax, that is, a national sales tax.

The Townsend Plan attracted a great many followers despite the fact that responsible fiscal leaders pointed out that if by some remote chance it did go into operation, half the national income would be required to take care of about nine million needy old people. Nevertheless, the Townsendites and their curious crusade were a definite political force in the mid-1930s, attracting several million followers. In fact it was not until 1937 that the movement began to die.

There were many other end-poverty plans proposed during this period. One was the somewhat cynical "Thirty Dollars Every Thursday" plan, which also promised free ham and eggs to all of its members. But by far the most politically potent scheme was the Share-Our-Wealth program cooked up by the United States Senator from Louisiana, Huey "Kingfish" Long.

The Share-Our-Wealth plan had an immediate appeal to the vast millions of unemployed, since it was based on redistributing the nation's private fortunes. Senator Long offered his plan with several variations, but it always included the following basic points: All individual inheritances would be limited to five million dollars; personal fortunes would be limited to eight million dollars; individual incomes in excess would be confiscated by the government to be redistributed among the people in the form of a free house, automobile, and radio to every family, plus an annual income of two thousand dollars. Long also proposed free college education for all young people and pensions for the aged.

Although most economists laughed at the Share-Our-Wealth program, millions of poor people across the nation rallied to Huey Long's cause, and thousands of Share-Our-Wealth clubs were formed. On the strength of such support Senator Long began to dream of becoming President. His assassination on

September 8, 1935, in a corridor of the Louisiana state capitol building in Baton Rouge by a local physician, Dr. Carl Austin Weiss, ended Long's dreams of glory, as well as the Share-Our-Wealth movement.

Both President Roosevelt and Frances Perkins believed that the welfare of the nation's wage earners should be protected by unemployment and old-age insurance. What stood in the way of such insurance was America's long tradition of self-reliance. Since pioneer days, Americans had taken a fierce pride in their ability to stand on their own feet and not ask for financial assistance from their government. Now, however, the worst economic depression in the nation's history had made most people modify this independent attitude.

Young men and women realized that a desire to work did not necessarily create jobs. Older people recognized the harsh truth that they could suddenly lose their jobs and be face to face in their old age with disastrous economic insecurity. It was this climate of opinion that caused many people to become interested in the various crackpot panaceas to eliminate poverty and unemployment and to provide for the aged. President Roosevelt and Frances Perkins realized that it was time for a sane unemployment and old-age insurance proposal.

In June 1934, FDR appointed Frances Perkins as the head of the Committee on Economic Security. The

End of the New Deal Honeymoon

executive director of her committee was Professor Edwin Witte. The other members included Henry Morgenthau, Jr., Homer Cummings, Henry Wallace, and Harry Hopkins. Arthur Altmeyer, Assistant Secretary of Labor and later commissioner of Social Security, coordinated the work of the committee and guided the bill through congressional hearings.

Frances Perkins went to work immediately to prepare legislation for presentation to Congress. Recalling her days in Albany when she had succeeded in getting bills passed by the New York state legislature, she again used experts for aid and advice. She called on Washington economists, statisticians, insurance executives—any and all professional men and women whose training and experience would prove valuable in preparing social insurance legislation and in convincing Congress of the need for such insurance. She also received valuable assistance from a twenty-three-member advisory council appointed by President Roosevelt to represent labor, industry, and the general public.

The deadline for presenting the legislation to Congress was early in 1935. As the deadline approached, Frances Perkins grew more and more fearful that the approval Congress had so far given almost all the New Deal measures would be withheld. The bill that was being prepared was, she knew, revolutionary. If it became a law, it would be the first basic federal social-welfare legislation in the history of the country.

FDR was reassuring, however. "Frances," he said, "every man, woman, and child in the country *has* to be guaranteed genuine security, a reasonable amount of leisure, and a decent living throughout their lives. You know it, I know it, and I think you'll find that the Congress knows it."

Frances Perkins' fears were unfounded. Despite its revolutionary nature, the Social Security Act was passed by both houses of Congress and placed on the President's desk for his signature by August 1935. The legislation had been sponsored in Congress by one of FDR and Frances Perkins' old friends from New York, Senator Robert Wagner. When President Roosevelt signed the bill, he called it, "The cornerstone in a structure which is being built but is by no means complete." He also paid glowing thanks to Frances Perkins and Senator Wagner for their efforts in behalf of the bill.

The Social Security Program, which began in 1935, was a blanket plan that offered protection to needy old people through pensions and public aid; it also promoted unemployment insurance throughout the nation, and had provisions for the care of the blind, the care of dependent children, and expanded the state public-health services. After the act was passed, Frances Perkins pointed out, "We would have had national health insurance, too, but we couldn't get our

End of the New Deal Honeymoon

data together in time." Old-age health insurance was to come, of course, but not for another thirty years.

Social Security benefits have been expanded in many ways since 1935. Almost immediately after the act's passage, however, its benefits began to be felt. Before the passage of the bill less than 5 percent of the aged received payments from retirement funds. Most old people had to be supported by their families or by various charities. Today almost 75 percent of the aged receive payments from social insurance and related benefits.

Among the changes later made in the Social Security Act was one that advanced the initial payment of monthly benefits from 1942 to 1940. A retired legal secretary, Ida Fuller of Ludlow, Vermont, became the first old-age insurance beneficiary when she received Social Security check number 00-000-001 on January 31, 1940. In almost half a century there would be nearly forty million beneficiaries.

Certainly one of the greatest strides forward accomplished by the Social Security Act was in aid to the unemployed. It helped establish a federal-state system of unemployment insurance. By offering certain tax benefits, it encouraged the individual states to set up systems of unemployment insurance along broad federal standards. Before the Social Security Act was passed, only Wisconsin had such an unemployment insurance law. Today all states do.

The Social Security system, however, has not been without its problems. One of its major difficulties has been the fact that within recent years it has shown constant deficits—more money is being paid out annually than is being taken in from employee payroll deductions and employer contributions. This means that some better means of financing the system will have to be found to keep it from going bankrupt. Several Presidents and the Congress have struggled to put Social Security back on a sound economic footing and there is little reason to doubt that they will eventually succeed.

A second major problem has to do with the relief or welfare program in general and with specific parts of the Social Security system.

The New Deal planners regarded all parts of their welfare program as stopgap measures. They did not think that welfare would or should become a permanent way of life for the nation, although that is pretty much what it has become. FDR himself said, "A permanent program for the poor is a poor program."

An example of how such stopgap measures have gotten out of hand has to do directly with the Social Security Act. When this act was passed, one of its virtually unnoticed parts was called Aid to Dependent Children (ADC). This clause said that the federal government would supplement aid that was then being paid by some states to mothers with dependent children. What FDR and Frances Perkins had specifically in mind was temporary help to the poor families of deceased coal miners. They believed the need for this aid would soon end when such families began to receive benefits from the new survivors' insurance program, which was also part of Social Security. But this did not happen. Instead, ADC need grew tremendously.

The original appropriation for ADC was twenty-five million dollars. In the late 1970s ADC payments amounted to ten billion dollars a year, and the end was not in sight. This, too, is a problem with which several Presidents and the Congress have grappled, with only partial success. Certainly solutions will be found, but the overall problem is not a minor one, as indicated by the fact that today all welfare costs amount to some sixty billion dollars a year.

CHAPTER TEN

The Supreme Court Fight

WHEN FDR RAN for reelection in 1936, most big businessmen and the well-to-do were against him. Most farmers, however, as well as the average working man and woman, were for him. Those who opposed Roosevelt said he was trying to become a dictator and turn America into a Fascist state, as Hitler and Mussolini had done in Germany and Italy.

One of the reasons that big business opposed FDR was the fact that the New Deal greatly encouraged the growth of the labor movement. Before the NRA was declared unconstitutional, more than a million new workers had joined labor unions. When certain employers refused to recognize these unions, many employees refused to work. Strikes and violence over union recognition and collective bargaining became widespread.

After the NRA was declared unconstitutional, the New Deal administration sponsored a bill called the National Labor Relations, or Wagner, Act, so called because it was introduced by Senator Robert Wagner —the man who also introduced the Social Security Act.

With the passage of the Wagner Act on July 5, 1935, workers no longer had to strike for union recognition and the right to collective bargaining. Unions continued to expand rapidly, union membership growing from about two and a half million in 1933 to some six million at the end of FDR's first term in office. But strikes continued. And they grew in size and violence as the unions grew. These strikes were held over wages and working conditions as well as fringe benefits such as health insurance. Big business claimed FDR and his New Deal were responsible for the strikes, which threatened democracy.

Despite big business opposition, however, on November 3, 1936, Franklin Roosevelt was reelected President in the biggest landslide victory since 1820 when James Monroe defeated John Quincy Adams by a margin of 231 electoral votes to 1. Roosevelt and his running mate—again it was John Nance Garner of Texas—defeated Alfred M. Landon of Kansas and

Franklin Knox of Illinois, 523 electoral votes to 8. Winning by a plurality margin of more than eleven million votes, FDR carried forty-six states, Landon two—Maine and Vermont. Up to that time a popular saying was, "As Maine goes, so goes the nation." After the election FDR's campaign manager, James Farley, wisecracked, "As Maine goes, so goes Vermont."

FDR and his New Dealers regarded this overwhelming victory as the public's stamp of approval on their efforts, and they were more determined than ever to continue the New Deal program. But troubles on the labor front also continued, and Congress was becoming more and more reluctant to rubber-stamp additional New Deal measures. This period between the end of the New Deal honeymoon and the start of World War II in Europe has often been referred to as the end of the first and the start of the second New Deal.

Even after FDR's landslide reelection, however, the administration's problems with strikes continued. First there was a series of "sit-down" strikes in 1937 that spread from the rubber-tire and automobile plants in Ohio and Michigan to other areas. The sit-down strike was a new technique adopted by workers who not only refused to work but also refused to leave the factories in which they were supposed to be working. Many responsible officials regarded the sit-down strike as illegal, claiming that the workers were unlaw-

The Supreme Court Fight

fully occupying property they did not own.

But legal or illegal, the sit-down technique resulted in important concessions to workers in an Akron, Ohio, rubber plant. From there the fadlike sit-down movement spread to the Ford and General Motors plants in Detroit and elsewhere throughout the nation. Also in 1937 there were threatened walkouts by laborers in the independent steel companies—Republic, Inland, and Youngstown Sheet and Tube.

Frances Perkins made valiant efforts to pacify this industrial strife, but her efforts were not always successful. American Federation of Labor President William Green was especially difficult, stating flatly that "the A. F. of L. will have no part of Madame Perkins' suggestions for compulsory acceptance of the Labor Department's decisions about arbitration."

Finally FDR suggested that Frances Perkins turn over many of the labor problems to several of her assistants. The men she and FDR picked to bring peace to the strike-torn steel mills were ideal for the job. They included Charles P. Taft, whose father, William Howard Taft, had been the twenty-seventh President of the United States; Lloyd Garrison, former chairman of the National Labor Relations Board; and Edward McGrady, the Labor Department's most accomplished troubleshooter.

During the course of the next several years these men managed to bring a certain degree of order out of the chaotic labor situation of the late 1930s. But serious labor trouble did not really end until America's entry into World War II.

All in all, 1937 was just not a good year for FDR and his New Deal. In addition to serious labor problems—or perhaps partially as a result of them—a kind of "mini-Depression" struck the nation. All of the economic gains that the New Deal administration had fought so hard for were suddenly threatened as unemployment again rose and the stock market plunged to new lows. And to make matters worse, FDR himself made one of the few truly major blunders of his Presidency—he attempted to change the structure of the Supreme Court.

Even before he was reelected, FDR had been toying with ideas of how he could somehow create a Supreme Court that would render more favorable decisions on the constitutionality of New Deal legislation. The Court had knocked down the NRA and the AAA, and had also ruled unfavorably against several other minor New Deal measures. Any day now FDR expected the Court to declare the Social Security Act and the National Labor Relations Act unconstitutional also. These two measures, he believed, were absolutely essential to the future well-being of the nation.

What was needed, FDR decided, was a more liberal Supreme Court. But the nine Supreme Court justices were appointed for life, and until one or more of them

The Supreme Court Fight

died or retired, FDR would have no chance to appoint any new, more liberal justices. The only alternative, FDR decided, was to increase their number to, perhaps, fifteen. But could he go about it without an amendment to the Constitution itself? Attorney General Homer Cummings supplied FDR with the answer —or what looked like the answer—and FDR leaped to take advantage of it. But he kept his plan secret right up to the last minute.

In his second inaugural address FDR gave no hint of what came to be called his "Court-packing plan." He did review the successes of the New Deal to date and asked, "Shall we pause now and turn our back upon the road that lies ahead?" The answer was, of course, *"no!"* Then he added:

> I see one-third of a nation ill-housed, ill-clad, ill-nourished. But it is not in despair that I paint for you that picture. I paint it for you in hope, because the nation, seeing and understanding the injustice in it, proposes to paint it out.
>
> We are determined to make every American citizen the subject of his country's interest and concern. . . .
>
> The test of our progress is not whether we add more to the abundance of those who have much, it is whether we provide enough for those who have too little.

Many people in the audience at his second inauguration fully expected FDR to attack the Supreme

Court, and when he failed to do so, they wondered just when the attack would come. They did not have long to wait.

Attorney General Cummings had long known of the President's desire to reshape the Supreme Court in a more liberal image. In December 1936, before the Inauguration, Cummings had found in the files of the Department of Justice a document dating back to 1913 that proposed the appointment of a new federal judge for every federal judge who had reached the retirement age of seventy and had not retired. The proposal had been prepared by James Clark McReynolds, who had been in 1913 the Attorney General but was now one of the most conservative members of the Supreme Court and a strong anti-New Dealer. McReynolds' early proposal, Cummings said, could be applied to *all* federal judges, which would include Supreme Court justices. FDR was so taken with Cummings' solution that he told the Attorney General to prepare immediately and secretly the necessary legislation to present to Congress.

Only a handful of FDR's aides knew about the judicial reform act of 1937 before it was presented to Congress early in February 1937. It exploded like a bombshell. The legislation proposed the appointment of a new or additional Supreme Court justice for each justice who had reached the age of seventy and had not retired. Everyone knew that several of the six Su-

The Supreme Court Fight

preme Court justices who were overage were also anti-New Dealers. The additional justices to be appointed by FDR would thus turn the Supreme Court into a "Roosevelt or New Deal Court." Such a law, if it were passed, would immediately change the nature of the federal government itself, giving the executive branch control of the judicial branch. The Founding Fathers had wisely decreed that these two branches of government, as well as the legislative branch, should be separate.

FDR had, of course, known that his proposed judicial reform act would cause a stir, but even he had not realized what a storm of protest it would create. His critics howled louder than ever, and even his friends opposed this bold move to change the American system of government. One of these friends, Chairman of the House Judiciary Committee Hatton Sumners, commented after hearing the proposal, "Boys, here's where I get off the New Deal boat." Even Vice-President Garner, always a loyal FDR supporter, held his nose in disgust when he first heard the proposal.

The nation's press also immediately and violently attacked the proposal, and public-opinion polls showed that the man in the street wondered if "maybe that man in the White House hasn't gone too far this time." Even a fireside chat to the American people defending his proposal failed to win the public to the President's side. National organizations such as the

Chamber of Commerce, the Liberty League, the Daughters of the American Revolution, the American Legion, and the National Association of Manufacturers all opposed this latest New Deal effort to "destroy democracy."

In the end, however, it was the Chief Justice of the Supreme Court, the old and venerable Charles Evans Hughes, who torpedoed the plan. Supreme Court justices had seldom been known to enter into any political controversies, so the fact that the Chief Justice himself had decided to do so now made his opinion on the FDR court-packing proposal even more effective.

In a letter to the Senate Judiciary Committee, Hughes took direct aim at the presidential message that had accompanied the proposed legislation. In his message FDR had cleverly implied that the Supreme Court was overburdened with work and was incapable of keeping up with its cases. "The personnel of the federal judiciary is insufficient," FDR's message said, "to meet the business before them." FDR had gone on to point out that there was a tendency on the part of judges to remain on the bench "far beyond their years of physical or mental capacity. A constant and systematic addition of younger blood will vitalize the courts and better equip them to recognize and apply the essential concepts of justice in the light of the needs and facts of an ever-changing world."

Hughes pointed out that no such problems of overwork or incapacity existed as far as the Supreme Court was concerned. The nine justices—whom FDR had often scathingly referred to as "the Nine Old Men"— were easily keeping up with their court calendar and handling all of the cases that appeared before them with time to spare. Thus there was no need for new or additional Supreme Court justices. As a matter of fact, Hughes added, additional justices might simply get in the way and impede the Court's efficiency rather than aid it.

But Hughes's most telling blow was aimed at the FDR suggestion that if there were fifteen justices the Court could split into two sections with each section acting independently of the other. This, Hughes observed with irrefutable logic, was clearly unconstitutional since Article III of the Constitution says, "The judicial power of the United States shall be vested in *one* Supreme Court."

After Hughes's letter was made public, FDR realized that his court-packing proposal was a lost cause. Actually, Senate hearings on the bill were to drag on until late July, but in the end it was soundly defeated.

Meanwhile, however, either pressured by the FDR scare tactics or "because it was beginning to see the light about liberal legislation," as FDR stoutly claimed, the Supreme Court suddenly began to rule in favor of a number of the most recent New Deal measures. First of all, the National Labor Relations Act was upheld; then the Social Security Act was approved, as well as several minor acts dealing with the nation's railway and farm workers. Then, on May 18, eighty-year-old Supreme Court Justice Willis J. Van Devanter, who had served on the Court for twenty-five years as a notorious conservative, announced his retirement. This opened the door for FDR to appoint a new and more liberal justice and thus probably obtain a liberal majority on the Court.

The man FDR chose was Hugo L. Black of Alabama. Black was known as a staunch New Deal supporter, but what was not at first known was that he had also been a member of the Ku Klux Klan in his native state. A new storm arose in the Senate over Black's appointment, centering around the question of whether Black should be allowed to become a Supreme Court justice charged with protecting the nation's civil liberties when he had belonged to a group like the Klan.

Black defended himself in a nationwide radio talk in which he confessed he had been a member of the Klan many years before, but he had resigned and never rejoined. He went on to say that he "had no sympathy whatever with any organization or group which, anywhere at any time, arrogates to itself the un-American power to interfere in the slightest degree with complete religious or racial freedom."

Black was confirmed shortly after his talk, and his concern with civil liberties soon became apparent in his numerous liberal opinions accompanying various Supreme Court decisions.

Then two other justices resigned—George Sutherland and Louis Brandeis, both of whom were past the retirement age of seventy—and a third justice died—Benjamin Cardozo. These were replaced by Solicitor General Stanley Reed, Chairman William O. Douglas of the Securities and Exchange Commission, and long-time FDR adviser and honorary father of the New Deal's Happy Hot Dogs, Felix Frankfurter. All of these men were cast in the New Deal mold, and thus, in a sense, FDR had won his Supreme Court fight. But his original devious method of attempting to change the structure of the Court and thus the structure of American government diminished FDR in the eyes of many of his previous admirers.

As a grim footnote to what can only be called the unfortunate year of 1937, a great air tragedy took place at Lakehurst, New Jersey. On May 6 the German dirigible *Hindenburg* caught fire and burned while trying to dock, killing thirty-five of the ninety-seven persons on board, as well as several ground crew members.

The size of the tragedy could not be measured so much by the number of casualties as by the fact that it virtually ended the use of lighter-than-air craft for passenger travel. Germany had pioneered in the military use of the lighter-than-air zeppelin in World War I, using it to bomb London. After the war, the German *Graf Zeppelin* had flown around the world in less than three weeks, and before it burned, the *Hindenburg* had made ten successful trans-Atlantic crossings between Germany and the United States.

However, although German dirigibles were no longer in use after the *Hindenburg* disaster, Germany continued to develop other advanced aircraft and aerial weapons. These would soon be raining down death and destruction from the sky not only over London but over other major cities, ushering in a second great world war.

CHAPTER ELEVEN

End of the New Deal

BEGINNING IN 1938, emphasis shifted away from domestic problems in the United States to foreign affairs. This shift marked the beginning of the end of the New Deal.

But before the New Deal died, FDR made a powerful, and vain, effort to consolidate his administration's hold on the government by purging the Democratic party of several of its leading figures who opposed the New Deal liberal philosophy. In a way this action was similar to the attempt to pack the Supreme Court, and it was equally unsuccessful as well as damaging to FDR's political image.

The President's motives were perhaps good. He

thought everybody in the Democratic party should be a liberal and everybody in the Republican party should be a conservative. This would give the voters a clear-cut choice as to which party they favored. As it was then, and still is today, both parties had liberal and conservative leaders, although as a whole the Democratic party was inclined to be liberal and the Republican party conservative. There was not much FDR could do about the Republicans, but as head of the Democratic party he felt he could and should rid it of conservatives.

The way FDR chose to go about his purge was to put his enormous presidential prestige and influence behind certain liberal Democratic members of the House and Senate who were up for reelection in the fall of 1938 and oppose those who had voted against some of the New Deal measures. Both Farley and Garner tried to tell FDR that this would be political suicide. The Democratic party's job was to elect Democrats and not pick and choose among them at the state level. Such intervention by FDR, they pointed out, would simply anger a number of representatives and senators and set the whole Congress against him. But FDR refused to heed Farley's and Garner's advice. In the end this led to a serious break between the President and these two valuable friends and colleagues.

In a fireside chat late in June 1938, FDR pointed out that the Congress had recently defeated a revised wage-and-hour bill that would have benefited every working man and woman. This bill had been defeated not by Republicans alone but by a coalition of Republicans and conservative Democrats. The country could not prosper, Roosevelt said, in the face of such negative action. The conservatives, FDR insisted, even though they were Democrats, had to be defeated in the fall elections.

During July and August, FDR actively campaigned in more than twenty state primary elections. Traveling across the country by train, he spoke out strongly for those candidates he favored and equally strongly against those he opposed. The height of this unprecedented effort was reached in Georgia, where FDR appeared on the same platform with but spoke against conservative Democrat Walter F. George, who had served in the Senate for almost twenty years. Afterward, George said to FDR, "Mr. President, I regret that you have taken this occasion to question my democracy and to attack my public record. I want you to know that I accept the challenge."

Mainly as a result of this incident, George was reelected by the largest majority he had ever received. Results were the same in almost every local election in which FDR intervened. His efforts succeeded only in making martyrs and easy winners out of almost everyone he opposed. Worse still was the fact that in the national elections in November the Republicans made substantial gains in both the House of Representatives and the Senate. The Democrats were still in the majority, but the margin was so slim that a handful of dissident Democrats could join with the Republicans and defeat any further New Deal measures. These elections all but spelled an end to the New Deal crusade.

Nevertheless, FDR continued to press for New Deal legislation, and after bitter fighting Congress went along with his proposals. This legislation included a federal crop insurance bill to protect farmers against losses from storms and natural disasters, an expansion of the TVA, and the building of other dams—Norris Dam on the Tennessee River and Bonneville and Grand Coulee dams on the Columbia River. Also in 1938 FDR finally got his revised wage-and-hour bill—the Fair Labor Standards Act. Under it wages were to begin at twenty-five cents an hour and rise in seven years to forty cents. The maximum work week was to be forty-four hours and drop to forty hours in two years.

In foreign affairs FDR had always been a devoted follower of President Woodrow Wilson, under whom he had served in World War I. He was a fervent seeker after world peace, a desire that would eventually lead to the founding of the United Nations as the successor to Wilson's unsuccessful League of Nations. FDR also believed in close friendship with Latin America and

Great Britain and in expanded world trade.

In his first inaugural address FDR had spoken of a "good neighbor" policy toward Latin America, but in the press of immediate Depression needs his words had temporarily gone unheeded. Nevertheless, under the New Deal FDR had insisted that the United States stop interfering in the internal political affairs of Latin American nations.

In 1934 the United States had rescinded the Platt Amendment which gave America the right to interfere in Cuba. That same year FDR ordered all United States marines to leave Nicaragua and Haiti. The New Deal Good Neighbor policy made FDR popular with Latin Americans, but increased his unpopularity with many American businessmen whose corporations had huge investments in Latin America and expected the government to protect them. This, FDR refused to do. A climax of sorts was reached in 1938 when Mexico seized the oil lands of several American companies and would not pay for them. FDR refused to interfere in the matter beyond lodging a mild protest.

The Good Neighbor policy also extended to Canada, where FDR was on extremely cordial terms. He worked with Canadian leaders to develop the Great Lakes–St. Lawrence Seaway, and in 1938 pledged to help defend it as well as the rest of Canada in case of enemy attack.

As a result of the Good Neighbor policy, most nations in the western hemisphere backed FDR's policies as World War II threatened. But the American people themselves refused to be alarmed—except to express great fear over the United States being drawn into the conflict. Since the end of World War I and its resulting disillusionment, the United States had been staunchly isolationist. FDR fought hard to alert and prepare the nation for war, but for many years isolationism continued to rule the land.

CHAPTER TWELVE

World War II Begins

ONE OF THE IRONIES of the New Deal was the fact that despite its heroic measures it never did end the Great Depression of the 1930s. It took World War II to do that by creating full employment in wartime factories, ending industrial strife by making strikes illegal under government fiat for the war's duration, and creating an Allied demand for all the food American farmers could produce.

At the height of the war only 670,000 persons were unemployed out of a total work force of sixty-six million men and women, whereas during 1932, a typical Depression year, there were at least twelve million unemployed out of a vastly smaller work force.

War had been brewing in Europe and in the Far East even before FDR was first elected President. While the United States was trying to solve its internal economic problems under President Hoover, Germany, Italy, and Japan were planning on solving their economic problems by foreign conquest.

Japan had made its first move to get more territory in 1931. It invaded Manchuria. The following year it invaded China. China called upon the League of Nations to take action against Japan, but the League did little about it. Hoover said he would refuse to recognize any territory that the Japanese gained by conquest. After FDR took office, Japan withdrew its troops from China for a time but fighting again flared up there in 1937.

In 1935 Benito Mussolini, Italy's dictator, sent troops into Ethiopia. Ethiopia's Emperor Haile Selassie turned to the League of Nations for help, but again little was done. The Ethiopian soldiers, equipped only with spears and other primitive weapons, were slaughtered by Italy's mechanized armed forces.

In the summer of 1936, civil war broke out in Spain in what really proved to be the opening European battle of World War II and that war's testing ground. At first all the nations of the world agreed to remain neutral in the conflict, but soon Italy and Germany sent troops to support the Fascist forces led by General Francisco Franco. Among the troops opposing

World War II Begins

Franco were volunteers from the United States, Great Britain, the Soviet Union, and many other anti-Fascist countries. These men fought in what was called the International Brigade.

In the fall of 1937, FDR reacted to these international threats of another world war by giving what he called his "Quarantine the Aggressors" speech. In it he said that all of the nations responsible for starting armed conflicts should be economically quarantined by the peaceful nations. But Americans refused to respond to his proposal. They opposed any kind of aggressive action, economic or otherwise. Public-opinion polls indicated that Americans were still overwhelmingly in favor of isolationism.

Shortly afterward Congress passed a permanent Neutrality Act, making it illegal to give loans, credits, or arms to any nation taking part in foreign conflict. FDR managed to spur Congress into passing a billion-dollar naval appropriations bill in 1938, to build a navy that could adequately protect both the Atlantic and Pacific coasts.

Meanwhile, Germany, Italy, and Japan proceeded with their foreign conquests. They formed an alliance that would be known as the Rome-Berlin-Tokyo Axis and ignored all pleas for maintaining the peace. It was finally Germany under Adolf Hitler, who had come to power in the same month and year that FDR's New Deal began, that precipitated the world conflict.

In March 1938, Hitler invaded Austria and made it part of Germany. He next threatened Czechoslovakia, since a part of it called the Sudetenland was already occupied mainly by Germans. FDR sent cables to both Hitler and Mussolini pleading for peace. The cables were ignored, and in the face of the threat of a general conflict breaking out, a conference of western Europe's leaders was hastily held at Munich, Germany. To appease Hitler, Germany was finally given the Sudetenland. A few months later Germany occupied the whole of Czechoslovakia.

As the European crisis mounted, America's isolationists grew even louder in their demands that the United States remain out of all foreign conflicts. Among the leaders of the isolationists was Colonel Charles A. Lindbergh, whose solo flight from New York to Paris in a single-engine monoplane, *The Spirit of St. Louis,* in May 1927 had made him one of the legendary American heroes.

Lindbergh was not only a legendary hero but also a somewhat contradictory one. In addition, he was one of the tragic figures of this period. Two years after his epic trans-Atlantic flight, Lindbergh had married Anne Morrow, daughter of Dwight W. Morrow, United States ambassador to Mexico. Their first child, Charles Augustus, Jr., was born in 1930. In 1932 the baby was kidnapped and murdered. The kidnapper and killer was not caught until 1934. He was Bruno

World War II Begins

Richard Hauptmann, an illegal alien from Germany living in New York City. In 1935 Hauptmann was tried and found guilty and sentenced to die in the electric chair. The sentence was carried out on April 3, 1936.

Meanwhile, to escape the publicity surrounding the tragedy, Colonel Lindbergh and his wife went to live in Europe. While they were in Europe Lindbergh became friendly with many of the top figures in European aviation, especially those in Germany. Hermann Goering, head of the German Luftwaffe, took Lindbergh on personal tours of aircraft factories and Luftwaffe air bases. Hitler and other German leaders also impressed Lindbergh with the superb organization and efficiency of the ever-growing Nazi war machine. So impressed was Lindbergh that he returned to the United States to report that he had seen "the wave of the future" in Germany and that rather than oppose the Nazis, Americans should be on their side. He also became one of the leaders of the America First Committee which publicly opposed American intervention in the war.

Many leading businessmen as well as a major part of the press also favored siding with Hitler. These men were not necessarily unpatriotic. They simply believed that Hitler was going to win any European war anyway and that America had better "start doing business with him" now. Interestingly, there were also a number of liberals who had backed FDR and the New Deal but were not in favor of getting involved in another war. Many of them were spokesmen for the nation's young people in high school and on college campuses who held frequent antiwar rallies and demonstrations and chanted their slogan: "Keep Us Out of War!"

Isolationism did not die down in the United States even when war began in Europe. On September 1, 1939, Hitler ordered his armies to attack Poland. At the time of the Munich appeasement agreement, Hitler had said he had no more territorial demands in Europe. In return both France and Great Britain had agreed that they would oppose any such additional German demands, by force if necessary. When Germany invaded Poland, France and Great Britain lived up to their agreements by declaring war on Germany.

The United States managed to remain neutral for twenty-seven months after the war in Europe began. Despite isolationist opposition, FDR almost single-handedly managed to turn America into what he described as "the arsenal of democracy." He persuaded Congress to repeal the arms embargo, and weapons and airplanes were sent to the French and British. Soon, "for defense purposes only," FDR was demanding millions of dollars in military appropriations and calling on American industry to produce fifty thousand planes. He also demanded a bigger army and navy, and in 1940 succeeded in starting a peacetime draft of men for the armed services.

World War II Begins

In 1940 FDR ran for an unprecedented third term as President. His opponent was a liberal Republican, Wendell Willkie. Despite the fact that no other American President had run for a third term, FDR was reelected with 55 percent of the popular vote and 449 electoral votes to 82 for Willkie.

Immediately after his reelection FDR went to work in earnest to prepare the nation for the war he knew America would soon be entering. In March of 1941 the Lend-Lease Act became law. It allowed the President to "sell, transfer title to, exchange, lease, lend, or otherwise dispose of war materials to countries whose defence was vital to American security." Britain's Prime Minister Winston Churchill called Lend-Lease "a supreme act of faith and leadership."

To protect the overseas shipment of lend-lease materials, American destroyers began patrolling the North Atlantic—an act just short of war.

In the Pacific, events were also leading to war. Convinced that Germany would defeat France and Great Britain, Japan set out to conquer Southeast Asia. When the United States protested Japan's seizure of French Indochina (today's Vietnam, Laos, and Cambodia) and threat to Burma, the Dutch East Indies, and the Philippines, the Japanese sent several diplomats to Washington to negotiate. While these negotiations were being carried on, the Japanese navy and air force made a surprise attack on Pearl Harbor, Hawaii, on December 7, 1941. The next day FDR, describing the Japanese attack as "a day that will live in infamy," requested Congress to declare war on Japan, Germany, and Italy. Congress quickly complied.

The New Deal crusade was now indeed over. The crusade against the Axis Powers for world freedom had just begun.

Bibliography

Adams, Henry H., *Harry Hopkins*, G. P. Putnam's Sons, New York, 1977.

Allen, Frederick Lewis, *Since Yesterday 1929–1939*, Harper & Brothers, New York, 1939, 1940.

Bird, Caroline, *The Invisible Scar*, David McKay Co., New York, 1966.

Bishop, Jim, *FDR's Last Year*, William Morrow & Co., New York, 1974.

Boardman, Fon W., Jr., *The Thirties*, Henry Z. Walck, Inc., New York, 1967.

Brogan, Denis W., *The Era of Franklin D. Roosevelt*, Yale University Press, New Haven, 1950.

Coffey, Thomas M., *The Long Thirst*, W. W. Norton & Co., New York, 1975.

Degler, Carl (ed.), *The New Deal*, Quadrangle Books, Chicago, 1970.

Filler, Louis (ed.), *The Anxious Years*, G. P. Putnam's Sons, New York, 1963.

Hurd, Charles, *When the New Deal Was Young and Gay*, Hawthorn Books, Inc., New York and London, 1965.

Kirkland, Winifred and Frances, *Girls Who Became Leaders*, Harper & Brothers, New York, 1932.

Lawson, Don, *The United States in World War I*, Abelard-Schuman, New York, 1963.

———, *The United States in World War II*, Abelard-Schuman, New York, 1963.

———, *Famous American Political Families*, Abelard-Schuman, New York, 1965.

———, *Frances Perkins, First Lady of the Cabinet*, Abelard-Schuman, New York, 1966.

Leighton, Isabel (ed.), *The Aspirin Age,* Simon & Schuster, New York, 1949.

Lindley, Ernest K., *The Roosevelt Revolution,* Viking Press, New York, 1933.

Long, Huey P., *Every Man A King,* Quadrangle Books, Chicago, 1961.

Moley, Raymond, *The First New Deal,* Harcourt, Brace & World, Inc., New York, 1966.

Perkins, Frances, *The Roosevelt I Knew,* Viking Press, New York, 1946.

Phillips, Cabell, *From the Crash to the Blitz, 1929–1939,* The New York Times Co., New York, 1969.

Roosevelt, Franklin D., *Looking Forward,* John Day Co., New York, 1933.

Sherwood, Robert E., *Roosevelt and Hopkins,* Harper & Brothers, New York, 1948.

Tugwell, Rexford G., *Roosevelt's Revolution,* Macmillan Publishing Co., New York, 1977.

Index

acreage-allotment plan, 81–82
Adams, John Quincy, 115
Addams, Jane, 58
aged:
  EPIC and, 105–106
  insurance for, 108–111
  Long's policy on, 107
Agricultural Adjustment Act (AAA), 51–52, 78, 80–81
  as unconstitutional, 79, 90–91, 118
Agriculture Department, U.S., 78, 80–84
Aid to Dependent Children (ADC), 112–113
Algren, Nelson, 101
Altmeyer, Arthur, 109
America First Committee, 137
American Federation of Labor (A.F. of L.), 60, 117
American Guide series, 101–102
American Legion, 122

antitrust laws, 55, 86, 90
Army, U.S., 15–16, 85
  CCC and 50, 61, 63, 64–65
Austria, 136
automobile plants, 14–15, 116–117

Babson, Roger, 10
Banking Act, 55–56
banks, 21, 36
  bank-holiday proclamation and, 43–49
  FDIC and, 55–56
  stock market and, 8, 10, 20, 48–49
Baruch, Bernard, 85
Belgium, 17
Benton, Thomas Hart, 102
Berle, Adolf A., Jr., 37
Black, Hugo L., 124–125
Black Thursday (October 24, 1929), 1, 10–11
Blue Eagle, 54, 55, 88
Bonus Army, 15–16, 19
"boondoggle," coining of, 97–98

INDEX

Brain Trust, 37–38, 43, 84, 86
Brandeis, Louis, 125
breadlines, 13
Burma, 139
businesses:
FDR opposed by, 53, 114–115, 131
Hitler as viewed by, 137
NRA and, 86–91
Byrnes, James F., 38

call money, 8
Campobello Island, 25, 29
Canada, 131
Cardozo, Benjamin, 125
Cermak, Anthony, 34–35
chain-letter craze, 103–105
Chamber of Commerce, 122
Chase, Stuart, 33
Cheever, John, 101
China, 134
Christadora House, 94
Churchill, Winston, 139
Civilian Conservation Corps (CCC) Reforestation Relief Act, 49–50, 82, 101
Perkins and, 56, 60–62, 63–65
Civil Works Administration (CWA), 50, 97, 98, 100
collective bargaining, 87, 115
college enrollments, NYA and, 101
Committee on Economic Security, 108–109

Congress, U.S., 20, 34, 81, 128
economic assistance legislation and, 18, 43, 46, 49–56, 87, 91, 92–93, 98–102, 108–113, 130
House Appropriations Committee of, 93
judicial reform act and, 120, 121, 122
naval appropriations bill in, 135
Neutrality Act and, 135
New Deal opposition in, 116
NRA and, 55, 87
Senate Judiciary Committee of, 122
social insurance legislation and, 109–110, 112, 113
veteran insurance policies and, 15
wage-and-hour bill in, 128–129, 130
World War II declaration by, 140
Constitution, U.S., 6, 119, 123
Coolidge, Calvin, 4–5, 7
Court-packing plan, 119–123, 127
Cox, James M., 28
Cuba, 131
Cummings, Homer S., 38, 109, 119, 120
Czechoslovakia, 136

144

Index

dams, 51, 53, 130
Daniels, Josephus, 27–28
Daughters of the American Revolution, 122
de Kooning, William, 102
democracy, 17
Democratic party, 27–28, 96
   elections of 1930s and, 20–22, 34
   FDR purge of, 127–130
   World War I and, 4
Depression, *see* Great Depression
Dern, George, 38
Douglas, William O., 125
dust-bowl crisis, 82–84
Dutch East Indies, 139

Economy Act, 46
education, Long on, 107
Eighteenth Amendment, 6
Eisenhower, Dwight D., 16
Emergency Banking Act, 46
End Poverty in California (EPIC), 105–106
Enterprise, 51
Ethiopia, 134

Fair Labor Standards Act, 130
Farley, James A., 22, 38–39, 116, 128
farmers, farming, 7, 12, 14, 18, 21, 78–84
   AAA and, 51–52, 78, 80–81, 90–91
   as FDR supporters, 114
   federal crop insurance bill for, 130
   World War I and, 2–3
   World War II and, 133
Farm Holiday Association, 14
Federal Art Project, 102
federal crop insurance bill, 130
Federal Deposit Insurance Corporation (FDIC), 55–56
Federal Emergency Relief Act, 50–51
Federal Emergency Relief Administration, 83, 92
   Hopkins vs. Ickes in, 96–99
   two parts of, 95
federal food-relief programs, 13, 52
Federal Music Project, 102
Federal Reserve banks, 48
Federal Reserve Board, U.S., 10
Federal Theater Project, 102
Federal Trade Commission, 86
Federal Writers' Project, 101–102
fireside chats, 47–48, 121, 128–129
Five Year plans, 54
Ford automobile plants, 14–15, 117
foreign markets, 2, 7

INDEX

France, 4, 17, 138, 139
Franco, Francisco, 134–135
Frankfurter, Felix, 80, 125
Frankfurter's Happy Hot Dogs, 80–81, 84, 90, 92
French Indochina, 139
Fuller, Ida, 111

Garner, John Nance, 22, 24, 33, 34, 115, 121, 128
Garrison, Lloyd, 117
George, Walter F., 129
Georgia Warm Springs Foundation, 31
Germany, 4, 28, 39, 64, 114, 125–126, 134, 135, 136, 140
Goering, Hermann, 137
gold, FDR legislation and, 44, 46
Good Neighbor policy, 131–132
Graf Zeppelin, 126
Grapes of Wrath, The (Steinbeck), 83
Great Britain, 4, 131, 135, 138, 139
Great Depression, 2, 12–22
  income and, 14
  starvation and, 21
  unemployment and, 12, 13, 21, 36, 49–55
  violence in, 14–15
  as worldwide, 39
  see also New Deal
Great Lakes–St. Lawrence Seaway, 131

Great Plains, 52
  CCC and, 50
  dust-bowl crisis and, 82–84
Green, William, 60, 62–63, 117

Haile Selassie, 134
Haiti, 131
Harding, Warren G., 3–4, 28, 39, 79
Hauptmann, Bruno Richard, 136–137
Hindenburg, 125–126
Hitler, Adolf, 39, 64, 114, 135–136, 137, 138
Hoover, Herbert, 4–5, 9–10, 13, 15–20, 134
  background and personality of, 16–18
  Bonus Army and, 15–16, 19
  economic beliefs of, 17–18
  1932 campaign of, 33–34
  renomination of, 21–22
  Roosevelt and, 36–37
Hoover Dam, 51
Hoover Pullmans, 19
Hoovervilles, 16, 19
Hopkins, Harry, 83, 92–95, 96–99, 109
  background of, 93–94
  WPA and, 99, 102
Howe, Louis McHenry, 22, 41

146

Index

Hughes, Charles Evans, 40, 122–123
Hull, Cordell, 38
Hull House, 58
Hyde Park, 27, 28

Ickes, Harold L., 38, 95–99, 102
  background of, 95–96
  nicknames of, 95
inheritances, Long on, 107
insurance, 111, 130
  FDIC and, 55–56
  old-age, 108–111
  unemployment, 108–111
Interior, U.S., Department of the, 96
International Apple Shippers' Association, 13
International Brigade, 135
investment trusts, 9, 11
isolationism, 4–5, 132, 135, 136, 137–138
Italy, 114, 134, 135, 140

Japan, 134, 135, 139–140
Johnson, Hugh ("Ironpants"), 37, 38, 81, 98, background and personality of, 84–85
  NRA and, 78–79, 86–90
Johnson, Lyndon Baines, 101
judicial reform act, 120–123
Justice Department, U.S., 120

Key West, Fla., 100
Kieran, James, 38
Knox, Franklin, 116
Ku Klux Klan, 124

Labor Department, U.S., 117
  Children's Bureau of, 61
  Federal Employment Service of, 61–62, 63
labor unions, 60, 62–63, 87
  NRA and, 114–115
  Wagner Act and, 115
LaFollette, Robert, 96
Landon, Alfred M., 115
Latin America, 130–132
League of Nations, 4, 28, 130, 134
Lend-Lease Act, 139
Liberty League, 122
lighter-than-air craft, 125–126
Lindbergh, Anne Morrow, 136–137
Lindbergh, Charles A., 136–137
Lindbergh, Charles Augustus, Jr., 136
Link, Robert H., 97–98
Lippmann, Walter, 24
Little White House (Warm Springs, Ga.), 31
Long, Huey ("Kingfish"), 107–108
Luftwaffe, 137

MacArthur, Douglas, 16, 85
McGrady, Edward, 117
McReynolds, James Clark, 120
"made work," 100
Manchuria, 134
manufacturing, 3, 5, 7, 12, 122
Mellon, Andrew W., 9–10
Mexico, 131
minimum wage, 63
Moley, Raymond, 33, 37, 41, 78, 85
Monroe, James, 115
Morgan, J. P., Company, 9
Morgenthau, Henry, Jr., 39, 109
Morrow, Dwight W., 136
Munich appeasement agreement, 138
Muscle Shoals, Ala., 52
Mussolini, Benito, 114, 134, 136

National Association of Manufacturers, 122
National Industrial Recovery Act (NIRA), 53–55
National Labor Relations Act, 115, 118, 123–124
National Labor Relations Board, 117
National Recovery Administration (NRA), 51, 54–55, 78, 84–91
labor unions and, 114–115
planned economy and, 54–55
as unconstitutional, 55, 79, 90, 114–115, 118
National Youth Administration (NYA), 100–101
Native Son (Wright), 102
naval appropriations bill (1938), 135
Navy, U.S., 27, 28
Neutrality Act, 135
New Deal, 2, 11, 43–132, 133
first, 43–113, 116
"First Hundred Days" of, 43–56, 103
labor movement growth under, 114–115
in 1937, 116–126
origin of term, 33
second, 116–132
see also specific legislation
New Deal, A (Chase), 33
New York Consumer's League, 57
New York State Employment Service, 61
New York's Temporary Emergency Relief Administration, 94
Nicaragua, 131
Nineteenth Amendment, 6
normalcy, 4–6

O'Connor, Basil, 37
"Old Age Revolving Pensions," 106–107

Index

Overseas Highway, 16, 51

Patton, George S., Jr., 16
Pearl Harbor, 139–140
Perkins, Frances, 39, 56, 57–65, 81, 90
   background of, 57–59
   Hopkins and, 93, 94
   insurance and, 108–110, 113
   minimum wage and, 63
   1937 industrial strife and, 117
   NRA and, 78
   work week length and, 58, 59, 87
Philippines, 139
Pittman, Key, 38
Platt Amendment, 131
Poland, 138
polio vaccine, 31
Pollock, Jackson, 102
poverty, panaceas for, 103–108
press, 121, 137
prices, NRA and, 54–55
processing tax, 81, 90–91
Progressive party, 96
prohibition, 6–7
protective tariffs, 5
Public Works Administration (PWA), 51, 96, 97
Pullman, George, 19

radio, FDR's use of, 40–41, 47–48, 121, 128–129

Reconstruction Finance Corporation (RFC), 18
Reed, Stanley, 125
Republican party, 96, 129
   as conservative, 128
   elections of 1930s and, 20, 21–22, 129–130
   World War I and, 4–5
Resettlement Administration, 83–84
Rome-Berlin-Tokyo Axis, 135, 140
Roosevelt, Anna Eleanor (daughter), 26, 29
Roosevelt, Eleanor (wife), 26, 84
Roosevelt, Elliott (son), 29
Roosevelt, Franklin Delano (FDR), 2, 11, 22–42
   background and career of, 25–29, 31–32
   Brain Trust of, 37–38, 43, 84, 86
   chain letters and, 105
   Democratic purge by, 127–130
   in election of 1932, 22–24, 32, 33–35
   in election of 1936, 114, 115–116
   in election of 1940, 139
   first Cabinet of, 38–39, 43
   first inauguration of, 36, 39–42
   foreign affairs and, 130–132, 134–136, 138–140
   as governor, 20, 32

INDEX

Roosevelt, Franklin D. *(cont.)*
  Hoover and, 36–37
  Hopkins and, 92, 94–95
  infantile paralysis of, 24, 29–31
  Perkins and, 58–61, 108–110, 113, 117
  "Quarantine the Aggressors" speech of, 135
  second inaugural address of, 119
  Supreme Court and, 118–125
  World War I role of, 28, 130
  World War I veterans and, 16
  see also New Deal
Roosevelt, Franklin Delano, Jr. (son), 29
Roosevelt, James (father), 25
Roosevelt, James (son), 26, 29
Roosevelt, John (son), 29
Roosevelt, Sara Delano, (mother), 25
Roosevelt, Theodore, 26, 33, 96
Roper, Daniel C., 38
Rosenman, Samuel I., 37
rubber-tire plants, 116–117

Scott, Sir Walter, 32
scrip, 45
Share-Our-Wealth plan, 107
Sheehan, William F. ("Blue-eyed Billie"), 27
Sherman Anti-Trust Act, 55
Sinclair, Upton, 105–106
sit-down strikes, 116–117
Smith, Alfred E., 22, 31–32
socialism, socialistic measures, 17, 53, 81–82
Social Security Act, 65, 103, 110–113, 115, 118, 124
soup kitchens, 13
Soviet Union, 54, 82, 135
Spain, 134
speakeasies, 6
Spirit of St. Louis, 136
Square Deal, 33
starvation, 17, 21
states, unemployment insurance and, 111
Steinbeck, John, 83
stock market, 1, 7–11, 13
  banks and, 8, 10, 20, 48–49
  buying on margin in, 7–8
  crash in, 1, 10–11, 12
  NRA and, 89
strikes, 116–117, 133
Sudetenland, 136
Sumners, Hatton, 121
Supreme Court, U.S., 118–125
  NRA and, 55, 90, 114–115
surpluses, 2, 13, 79, 90, 91
Sutherland, George, 125
Swanson, Claude A., 38

Taft, Charles P., 117
Taft, William Howard, 117
Tammany Hall, 27

150

Index

tariffs, protective, 5
taxes, 81, 91
   Townsend and, 106
Tennessee Valley Authority (TVA) Act, 52–53, 130
Texas, 101
"Thirty Dollars Every Thursday" plan, 107
Thoreau, Henry David, 41
Townsend, Francis E., 106
Townsend Plan, 106–107
trade associations, 87
Treasury Department, U.S., 46–47
Triangle Shirtwaist Company, 58–59
Truman, Harry, 93
Tugwell, Rexford Guy, 37
   AAA and, 78, 80–81
   background of, 79–80
   Resettlement Administration and, 83–84
Twenties (decade), 2–11
   economic problems in, 3, 7–11
   isolationism and, 4–5
   normalcy and, 4–6
   "silent depression" in, 3

unemployment, 3, 12, 13, 18, 21, 36, 136
   insurance, 108–111
   legislation on, 49–55, 86–91, 96–102, 103, 109–111
   panaceas for, 103–108
   World War II and, 133

unions, *see* labor unions
United Nations, 130

Van Devanter, Willis J., 124
veterans, 15–16, 46

wage-and-hour bill, 128–129, 130
Wagner, Robert, 110, 115
Wagner Act, *see* National Labor Relations Act
Wallace, Henry A., 38, 39, 109
   AAA and, 78, 80–81
   background of, 79
Wallace's Farmer magazine, 79
Wall Street, 8, 9, 12, 13
War Industries Board, 85
Weiss, Carl Austin, 108
Willkie, Wendell, 139
Wilson, Paul C., 59
Wilson, Susanna Winslow Perkins, 59
Wilson, Woodrow, 3, 4, 27, 28, 130
Wisconsin, unemployment insurance in, 111
Witte, Edwin, 109
women, 6, 39
Woodin, William H., 38, 39
Works Progress Administration (WPA), 50, 98–102
   Federal Writers' Project of, 101–102
   NYA of, 100–101

INDEX

work week, 58, 59, 87, 90
  NIRA and, 53
World War I, 2–5, 7, 52, 59, 130
  economic effects of, 2–3, 5, 7
  German dirigibles in, 126
  Hoover's role in, 17
  isolationism and, 4–5, 132
  Johnson's role in, 85
  nature of war and, 3–4
  veterans of, 15–16

World War II, 39, 50, 93, 101, 102, 116, 133–140
  CCC and, 65
  Good Neighbor policy and, 132
  labor trouble and, 118
  PWA and, 51
Wright, Richard, 101, 102

Yorktown, 51

Zangara, Giuseppe, 34

320.973
LAWSON D
FDR'S NEW DEAL